"This book is for anyone, no matter your situation. You will find out that God is able to do more than you would even dare to dream, despite hard times and setbacks. Clinton's practical steps will put you on the right journey for your life."

John V Thomas
Founder and Global Ambassador of Living Hope

"This is not just another self-help book. Clinton is a living testimony of Gods grace and in this book he shares powerful truths of how God can change your life and use you."

Neil Smith
Senior Pastor, King of Kings Baptist Church

"Inspirational. Life-changing. Easy to implement. A must-read to get you going towards your God-given destiny."

Josh Werner
Founder of BetterYouLiving

DARE TO DREAM

LIFT THE LID. AIM HIGH.
ATTEMPT GREAT THINGS
WITH GOD.

CLINTON J WERNER

Published Independently by

CJ Werner
P O Box 22535
Fish Hoek
Cape Town, 7974
South Africa

www.betteryouliving.com

In association with

PUBLISHING **DESIGN**

DEDICATION

This book is dedicated to my four sons,
Daniel, Josh, Elijah, and David.

Keep Lifting the Lid.
Dare to Dream.
Aim High.
Above all, keep Jesus
at the center.

For more information on international distribution,
email <u>team@betteryouliving.com</u>

For more information and templates, please refer to
our website and blog, <u>www.betteryouliving.com</u>

This book and other BETTER**YOU**LIVING resources
are available at
<u>www.betteryouliving.com</u>

66

But blessed are those who trust in the Lord and have made the Lord their hope and confidence. They are like trees planted along a riverbank, with roots that reach deep into the water. Such trees are not bothered by the heat or worried by long months of drought. Their leaves stay green, and they never stop producing fruit.

Jeremiah 17:7-8

CONTENTS

66

*Hope deferred
makes the heart sick,
but a dream fulfilled
Is a tree of life.*

Proverbs 13:12 NLT

Introduction
DARE TO DREAM
Your Best Days Are Ahead!

I am fortunate to live in Noordhoek, in the southern peninsula of Cape Town, nestled between two oceans. Cape Town truly is one of the most beautiful cities in the world, with sublime sandy beaches, incredible sunrises and sunsets, the iconic Table Mountain, and the spectacular Winelands. In summer, Cape Town blossoms. It is a must-visit city, voted as one of the top tourist destinations in the world.

While Cape Town's beauty is undeniable, inequality is rife. Homes in the suburbs and on the tourist strip are lovely. Still, we have numerous informal settlements where many live in shacks and survive on income way below the breadline.

According to government statistics, of the 3.7 million people living in Cape Town, the unemployment rate is at 24%, whilst amongst the youth, unemployment is at a shocking 31% (statssa.gov.za). This means that out of every ten young people looking for a job, only seven will find work, leaving the rest deflated, broke, and disillusioned.

Close to our home on the Cape Peninsula, we have a township called Masiphumelele, which means "let us succeed" in Xhosa. Masiphumelele, affectionally known as Masi, has around 26,000 residents. While some live in brick homes, many live in shacks.

A friend of mine recently surveyed the youth in Masi. He intended to see where the youth were at and how he could help them develop their entrepreneurial skills to see them become successful and soar. In his survey, he started by asking about their dreams and aspirations. While we both thought that the youth would be dreaming of one day...

- Becoming a CEO of a major listed company
- Becoming President and changing the world
- Aiming to run their own successful business
- Becoming a world-renowned athlete

We were left heartbroken and disturbed to hear the reality that while a few had dreams similar to above, the vast majority in the survey had very low expectations.

When asked about their future dreams and ambitions, the standard answers were mostly like this: I dream that one day I will be able to get a job as a...

- Domestic worker
- Gardener
- Garbage collector
- Postman

These young men and women had experienced such hard knocks in their lives. They were living with such a poverty mindset that they were not even able to dream, resulting in their hopes and goals for the future being extremely low.

Through my community and business interactions, I meet with people from all walks of life. One thing is clear: people from both the upper-most and gutter-most ends of society have stopped dreaming. Many have lost purpose and passion. Many are just going through the motions. Based on local and global responses from the blogs I write and the radio shows I present, many are disillusioned and feel down. I am sure that the pandemic and wars around the world have left many fearful and stressed out, too.

Additionally, high global inflation has caused the cost of living to skyrocket, leaving many cash-strapped and debt-ridden. This has left many feeling down and out.

I believe it is time to lift your head and dream again.

You may have let go of your dreams. Your outlook may be pessimistic. You may have lost vision for your future. Maybe you have lost hope.

I need to tell you that there is hope.

With God's help, you can turn your life around. You can get back up. He is the way maker. He can fix what is broken. This is the reason I have written this book – to help you get your life back with a new vision and to see you prosper.

Despite the chaos, there is hope. It is not how you start the journey that's important; it is how you finish the race. You can get back up. Dust yourself off. It is time for a fresh start.

I have broken this book down into three parts:

Part one: RISE UP

The aim of part one is to encourage you to dare to dream and to lift the lid. Using powerful illustrations as well as principles out of the Word of God, this section will motivate you to formulate a fresh vision, overcome setbacks, and arise.

Part two: THE PRACTICE

This section will give you the practical steps that you can apply to help you achieve your dreams. Starting with your dream, we will help you map out a plan. Unfortunately, even with a dream and a plan, many never end up following through on their dreams. This section, therefore, also includes a simple step-by-step strategy and an easy-to-follow blueprint to make it easy for you to stick to your plans until you see your dreams come to pass.

Part three: FINISHING STRONG

The final part of the book will help you break any limiting beliefs that may be sabotaging your dreams and holding you back from reaching your destiny. You will also be spurred on to keep moving forward, to go after your dreams, and to keep on pressing on until your dreams become a reality.

It is your time to **dare to dream.**
It is time to **reset your goals.**
It is time to **rekindle your passion.**
It is time to **aim high.**
It is time to **attempt great things with God.**
It is time to **live on purpose.**
It is time to **reignite your vision.**
It is time to **be fruitful.**
It is time to **get positioned** for God to
catapult you into your **destiny.**

Your **best days** are ahead of you.

PART ONE

RISE UP!

66

*But those who trust in the Lord
will find new strength.
They will soar high on
wings like eagles.*

Isaiah 40:31 NLT

Chapter 1

TIME TO FLY

It is Your Time to Soar Like an Eagle.

THE EAGLE

I heard a story about an eagle who thought he was a chicken.

When the eagle was a young eaglet, he fell out of his nest on a mountain ledge. A farmer happened to pass through the valley and found this injured eaglet. He took him back to his farm, where he raised it in the chicken coop.

The young eagle grew up with the chickens. He became like one of them. He lived like a chicken. He ate like a chicken. He believed he was a chicken.

One day, a man visited the farm. He was surprised to see the eagle strutting around the chicken coop, pecking at the ground, and acting like a chicken. This man was seriously bothered to see the king of all birds, who should be soaring the skies, just waddling around in the dirt of a chicken coop.

He asked the farmer if he could get this eagle to see himself as an eagle instead of a chicken. The farmer was keen to try anything to help him.

The man took the eagle and placed him on a fence. He then spoke to the eagle, "You are an eagle. Stretch out your wings and fly."

The eagle just looked around confused, first at the man, then at the farmer, and then down at the chickens. He jumped off the fence, went straight back to the chicken coop, and started pecking the ground.

The farmer said, "You see! Even though he looks like an eagle, inside, he is just a chicken."

This eagle was comfortable living like a chicken in his chicken coop.

But the man was really bothered. He asked the farmer if he could try something else. This time, he took the eagle out into the countryside, up the mountain, away from the farm and the chickens.

On a ledge at the top of the mountain, he raised the eagle and said, "It is your time to fly."

The eagle looked up. The sun was bright. The sky was blue. The eagle lifted his head and stretched out his majestic wings. He then let out a screech and took off into the sky.

He soared higher and higher, using his powerful wings to glide through the sky. That day, this majestic bird left his chicken coop for good. He began to soar. He was no longer a chicken. He had discovered his destiny. He was an eagle.

DON'T STAY IN THE CHICKEN COOP

We all face problems in life. It is easy to keep a positive attitude and keep going when the problem is small, but when we face a bigger crisis, it can be debilitating. Often, when we take a hard knock, it is not so easy to get back up. And when a barrage of setbacks hits us, it is sometimes easier to stay down, accept a position of compromise, and let go of your dreams and aspirations.

So many have let go of their God-given dreams and are groveling in the chicken coop of life instead of fulfilling the destiny and purpose for which they were created.

Today, I want to encourage you not just to accept the tough times as your lot in life. You can get back up. You can shake off the dust and rise again. No matter where you are today or what has happened, you can rise back up.

If life has thrown you lemons, you can let the disappointments and battles cause your life to become sour, or you can choose to rise and use the lemons to make lemonade.

God has called you to be an eagle, but so many are living like chickens, way below their potential and calling. So many have let go of their God-given destiny and are comfortable in the chicken coop while God wants them to soar. You can fly again.

FLY

It is time to soar.

Isaiah gives a picture of burnt-out and broken people, barely surviving and definitely not thriving. They were worn out and tired, just going through the motions, with no hope for the future.

God told his people through the Prophet Isaiah,

"How can you say the Lord does not see your troubles?" —Isaiah 40:27

Isaiah continued, *"He gives power to the weak and strength to the powerless."* —Isaiah 40:29

If you are weak and powerless, know that God can make you strong.

God went on and encouraged his people by saying, *"Even youths will become weak and tired, and young men will fall in exhaustion. But those who trust in the Lord will find new strength. They will soar high on wings like eagles. They will run and not grow weary. They will walk and not faint."* —Isaiah 40:30-31

God told His broken and weak people to lift their weary heads, to look to Him, and to wait on Him because He is willing and able to lift them up, right out of the garbage dump of life. And God can do the same for you!

Today, God is calling you to look to Him as your Saviour. Wait on Him. Trust Him. God can renew your strength. He is also willing and able to lift you up on wings like eagles so that you can soar high.

God is calling you to fly once again. He can mend your broken wings. He can lift you up. God doesn't want you to be a chicken, scratching around in the dust of the chicken coop, looking for worms, and pecking at the grain. He wants you to look to Him, to look up, lift the lid, fly, and soar. I believe that God wants to catapult you into your destiny.

HOPE

"'For I know the plans I have for you,' says the Lord. 'They are plans for good and not for disaster, to give you a future and a hope.'" —Jeremiah 29:11

This scripture was written to God's people who had let go of Him. They had turned their back on Him and had ended up in captivity, exiled to a land that wasn't theirs. They were barely surviving. Times were tough. They had let go of their dreams. They thought there was no hope and that this was their lot in life.

In the middle of their hopeless situation, with nothing to look forward to except misery and pain, God gave them this word through the Prophet Jeremiah. He told His wayward people that He still had a plan for their lives, a plan not to harm them but a good plan to give them hope and a brighter future.

God still has a plan for you too.

It is a plan to prosper you, not to harm you. It is a plan to give you hope and a brighter future.

RESTORE

God went on and said, *"'In those days when you pray, I will listen. If you look for me wholeheartedly, you will find me. I will be found by you,' says the Lord. 'I will end your captivity and restore your fortunes.'"* —Jeremiah 29:12-13

God told his people to turn back to Him, to listen to Him, and to seek Him with all their hearts. He promised that when they looked to Him, He would bring them out of their captivity and bring restoration.

This shows God's heart for His wayward people. Even though they had neglected God, He still reached out to them. When they were down and out, He lifted them up. He helped them dream again, lift the lid, set their sights once again on God first, and get their priorities right, with God at the center.

Although they were stuck in the chicken coop, God was about to launch them into their destiny.

You may find yourself in the chicken coop of life. You may have given up on your dreams. You may have taken so many hard knocks that you have let go of your destiny. You may be going through the motions. It's easy to get complacent and comfortable in the dirt of the chicken coop.

Your life may be dark and gloomy. You may feel weak and weary. You may have nothing to look forward to. You may be bitter with a sour taste in your mouth.

But God wants you to soar above the gloomy clouds. He wants you to let go of the hurt and pain. He wants you to dare to dream, aim high, lift the lid, and attempt great things with Him. So, don't cluck like a chicken. Soar like an eagle.

LIFT OFF

God is strong and mighty. He can revive your life. He can renew your strength. He can lift you up.

Psalm 113 says, *"Who can be compared with the Lord our God, who is enthroned on high? He stoops to look down on heaven and on earth. He lifts the poor from the dust and the needy from the garbage dump. He sets them among princes, even the princes of his own people!"* —*Psalms 113:5-8*

God sees all. He knows what is happening in your life. He wants to lift you up, out of the dust and garbage. He wants you to soar.

Look to Him.
Lift your weary head.
Dare to dream.
Aim high.
Lift the lid.
Attempt great things.
Fly.
Soar.

"Those who trust in the Lord will find new strength. They will soar high on wings like eagles. They will run and not grow weary. They will walk and not faint." —*Isaiah 40:30-31*

66

For I am about to do something new.
See, I have already begun!
Do you not see it?
I will make a pathway
through the wilderness.
I will create rivers
in the dry wasteland.

Isaiah 43:19

Chapter 2
A FRESH START

It is Your Time to Start Afresh.

No matter where you find yourself today, you can start afresh. You can begin again.

In life, we go through seasons.

King Solomon, known as the wisest man in the world in his generation, said, *"There is a time for everything and a season for every activity under the heavens." —Ecclesiastes 3:1*

You can start afresh regardless of where you find yourself today or what you are facing.

MY FRESH START

When I first started working in the corporate world in my early twenties, I had no money management skills. When I landed my first job, I was earning a good income. Thanks to the credit and store cards that banks and clothing retailers were eager to give me, I lived the high life, dressed up, and spent money on anything I liked. I rented a nice home. I bought a Toyota Conquest Sport Edition on finance, with all the cool fittings. I was living the good life. I had money, and it felt like I had a never-ending supply - that's until I maxed out my credit cards and realized that I had more month left than money! I decided to leave the company I worked for and joined one of the biggest insurance companies in South Africa as a financial advisor, with the aim of making more money to fund my empty lifestyle. At first, things went well. I contacted my friends and colleagues at my previous company and signed them on several insurance and investment products that brought in good money. I was living it up, in sin, without a care in the world.

Then, almost overnight, all hell broke loose. The old company where my friends worked, who were now my clients, closed down, leaving them jobless. Because they couldn't pay the premiums on their policies, their policies lapsed, leaving me with a heap of debt I needed to repay, and my income grounded to a halt.

Over the following three months, I had very little money coming in. My car ran on petrol fumes, I couldn't cover my rent, and I had the landlord breathing down my neck. I couldn't pay my car. The bank was calling me daily, demanding payment. The clothing stores I had cards with were also threatening me. The finance division at the bank wanted to take my car away. **I hid my car around the corner and avoided all their calls.** I had no cash flow. My credit cards were maxed out. I was left three months in arrears on my rent and was kicked out of my rented home. My car was four repayments behind. I owed the company I worked for a large amount of money due to the lapses, which they wanted back. They deducted 80% of the income I earned each month to recover this debt, leaving me with 20% to live on, which wasn't even enough to cover my fuel and food bill. The debt I owed to the company I worked for may not seem like much today, but thirty years ago, it was equivalent to buying a three-bedroom home in a middle-class suburb. I also owed tens of thousands on my credit cards. I was stressed out, to put it mildly. I was scared to answer the phone because it was always another creditor asking for money. I was practically bankrupt. Under the stress, my work suffered, and my commission income was reduced. I was left financially ruined. With poor financial wisdom and insufficient money to cover my basic living expenses, I didn't know where to turn.

It felt like I had a pile of bricks on my shoulders. It felt like I had this thick mist around my head. I was scared and worried. My mom was telling me to take it to God in prayer, but I saw this as my problem: I had created the debt, and it was my mess to fix.

But I hit rock bottom. I got to a stage where I could not take it anymore. One day, completely heartbroken, I fell on my knees and surrendered my burdens and debt to Jesus.

That day, I asked God to forgive me of my many sins. I surrendered my burdens to God. He did a supernatural work in my heart. **I literally felt the hand of God on my back.** I knew God loved me and that He had forgiven me. My debt was still there, but after praying, it felt like the mist had lifted, and I had peace in my heart. The heavy load seemed to be lifted off my shoulders.

My debt was still there, but I knew that Jesus was my provider and that He would see me through. A week later, I received a surprise refund from the taxman. This was a miracle. I was expecting a tax refund, and I followed this up with the tax revenue office. They had told me that my tax had not been assessed and that it would take at least a few months before the refund was processed. The next day, my accountant called to say he had gone to his P O Box and that there was a cheque from the tax man made out to me. It was the exact amount needed to settle my car and outstanding rent. God works in mysterious ways.

I knew God was with me. I had peace, and in the months and years that followed, God supernaturally provided for my needs, so much so that I could get through this.

This seriously difficult time ended up being a life-changing season, which was instrumental in growing my relationship with God. Why? Because I had to rely on Jesus.

During this time, I decided never to get back into debt again. With God's help and some discipline, I have turned my money situation around. While it took me a few years to get back on my feet, I was able to start afresh.

I am so thankful that this all happened before I was

married. Not only did I manage to settle all my debts with God's help, but by applying his wisdom, I have managed to turn my financial affairs around for the good. Today, I am married, and I have four sons, two of whom are in university. We have no bad debts that cause stress. Today, I have helped build up a good business, run a ministry, and have been allowed to host a radio program for nearly 30 years. Through my profession and the ministry opportunities that God has opened, I have had the privilege of helping many turn their lives around for the good and helping them dream again.

Over the past 30 years, I have set many goals and dreams for the future. Some of them have already materialized. For example, I dreamed of taking my family on an overseas holiday. I set the goals, implemented a strategy to save up the money, and was able to do this. As a family, we have many other goals that we have accomplished and many other goals that we hope to reach in the future. I have a goal to retire one day. My retirement planning remains on track. I had a goal of always setting sufficient disposable funds aside to cover emergency needs. When Covid hit, we were left standing because of the provision we had set aside. We are also busy planning our next family adventure.

With God, we have dared to dream, aimed high, and were able to set new goals. With God's grace and mercy, I was able to start afresh. Today, you can begin afresh and dream again too.

GOD HAS A GOOD PLAN FOR YOUR LIFE

God loves you. In the last chapter, we looked at how God has plans for his people: *"They are plans for good and not for disaster, to give you a future and a hope." —Jeremiah 29:11*

No matter what you have done or where you find yourself, God still has a plan not to harm you. He has a good plan to give you HOPE and a BRIGHTER FUTURE.

If you find yourself in captivity, seek Him.

If you find yourself living without God, I want to encourage you to return to Him again.

God has your best interest at heart. He wants you to succeed and be all you were made to be. God has a destiny for you to fulfill. He is for you and not against you. He can fix anything that is broken. He can make a way.

GOD CAN FIX IT

No matter where you find yourself currently, we are told, *"God causes everything to work together for the good of those who love God and are called according to his purpose for them." —Romans 8:28*

God can cause ALL THINGS to work out for the good. Trust Him. Hold onto Him.

It is easy to give up on your dreams when you take a series of hard knocks and when times are tough, but you need to have vision.

What are your God-given dreams? What are your goals? What are your plans?

God wants to see you succeed and fulfill your destiny. He wants to see you live on purpose and with passion.

INVITE GOD TO BE A PART OF YOUR JOURNEY

Don't go at your plans alone. Invite Jesus to be the center of your dreams and ambitions. He wants to help you set a winning strategy. He wants to see you succeed.

FRESH START

You can start afresh. You can begin again.

God has a good plan for you. Dream big dreams. Have vision. Set up a plan. Surrender your life and plans to God. He wants to do life with you. It's your time to...

- Dare to dream
- Aim high
- Attempt great things with God and for God
- Live on purpose and live with passion
- It is time to arise.

Will you put God first? Will you commit your plans to Him?

He wants to help you achieve your God-given destiny. He wants to lead and guide you on a new adventure. He wants to see you reach your goals. He wants you to be fruitful.

With God on your side, all things are possible, but there's one thing you need to do... JUMP!

66

Peter, suddenly bold, said,
'Master, if it's really you,
call me to come to you on the water.'
He said, 'Come ahead.'
Jumping out of the boat,
Peter walked on the water to Jesus.

Matthew 14:28-29 MSG

Chapter 3

JUMP!

Dare to Risk. Attempt Great Things.

Many think that fleas can fly. Well, I have news for you - they can't! They do not have wings. But fleas have the incredible ability to launch themselves up to 100 times their body length into the air. This means that they can jump up to 2 feet in height!

We are a lot like fleas in some regards. You and I have an incredible ability to do great things. Still, we often achieve way less than we are capable of because of the limiting beliefs brought on by our environment and those we hang out with.

THE FLEA IN THE JAR

Have you heard of the flea-in-a-jar experiment?

A scientist placed several fleas in a jar. Immediately, the natural reaction of each flea was to jump out of the jar. However, a lid was then placed on the jar. At first, the fleas went wild. They kept jumping and hitting their heads on the lid. But after a while, and after bumping their heads many times, the fleas learned the boundaries of the jar. They began to jump lower, just below the glass lid, so that they did not hit it.

After three days, the lid was taken off.

Guess what happened? Although these fleas had the ability to jump out of the jar, they didn't. Although they could have jumped out, they just stayed in the jar, jumping a little lower than the height of the lid.

It only took three days to teach these fleas to limit their beliefs and accept their new lot in life. With the lid removed, they could have launched into their freedom, but because they were so conditioned by their new boundaries, they were stuck in the jar.

The lid was no longer needed. The fleas had been conditioned to accept that they couldn't jump out any longer. These fleas never again jumped out of the jar. In fact, they never jumped past the level of the lid.

What is worse is that the experiment continued...

When the fleas in the jar had offspring, the new baby fleas learned their parent's limiting beliefs and followed in their footsteps, never jumping higher than the lid. The younger generation of fleas in the jar automatically followed the example of the other fleas and stayed within the bounds of the jar.

What a tragedy.

Unfortunately, this is a lot like how most people live today. We have been conditioned by our environment. We live in our own jars with lids we cannot see past, let alone jump out of. But it is time to go after your dreams and to jump.

Don't settle for a life in the jar. Launch out.

I am fully aware that it can be scary to jump out of your comfort zone when you don't know what is beyond the lid. It can seem daunting and dangerous, but what have you got to lose? Worst case, you bump your head!

Today, I encourage you to let go of your limiting beliefs. Dare to risk. It is time to lift the lid, jump out of your jar, and catapult into your destiny.

DON'T SETTLE FOR LESS

Don't say your dream is impossible. In your own strength, your dream may seem out of your reach, but I need you to know what Jesus said. He said, *"With God all things are possible." —Matthew 19:26*

WALK ON WATER

There is a story in the Bible where Jesus' disciples took a boat trip across the Sea of Galilee.

That morning, Jesus had heard the terrible news that John the Baptist had been beheaded. He was the one who came to prepare the way for Jesus' coming. He had also baptized Jesus in the River Jordan.

After hearing the heartbreaking news, Jesus just needed some alone time to mourn the death of his friend and spend some time with God. However, the crowds had come to look for Him. Although Jesus wanted to be alone, He spent the entire day ministering to the hurting and broken people. He then fed the crowd of 5000 men plus their families with a little boy's lunch, and after everyone had eaten all they could, there were still baskets left over.

It is amazing to see that Jesus is never too busy for you. He loves to heal and build people up. He loves to bless and provide for His people, and when He does, He always provides in abundance.

Jesus can also do the impossible! He can take the little and multiply it into lots.

After ministering to the crowd, Jesus sent his disciples on ahead while He stayed behind to pray. The disciples got in their boat and set off on their journey, while Jesus went up into the hills by himself to spend time with God in prayer.

While the disciples were out at sea, a storm arose unexpectedly in the early hours of the morning. We are told that *"the disciples were in trouble far away from land, for a strong wind had risen, and they were fighting heavy waves."* —Matthew 14:24

Jesus knew that they were struggling, and He set off to rescue them. There were no boats available, so what did Jesus do? He came to them, *"walking on the water."* —Matthew 14:25

Jesus can do all things. He can do the impossible. You can rest in Him. Today, if you feel stuck in your boat of life in the middle of a storm, call out to Jesus. He can rescue you.

I recently spent a few days at the Sea of Galilee. I heard a few stories of how storms can arise out of nowhere. By the way, I tried to walk on the water there. I couldn't, but I did swim in the sea.

"When the disciples saw Him walking on the water, they were terrified. In their fear, they cried out,

'It's a ghost!'" —*Matthew 14:26*

Remember, it is around 3 am. The wind is howling. It is still dark. The furious storm is rocking the boat, and they see this figure walking on the water. They are frightened, but then they hear the voice of Jesus, *"Don't be afraid. Take courage. I am here!"* —*Matthew 14:27*

Immediately, they knew they were safe. Their Savior was there. He had come, walking on the water, to rescue them. All of a sudden, the fear disappeared, and faith arose.

Then Peter called to Him, *"Lord, if it's really you, tell me to come to you, walking on the water."* — Matthew 14:28

Jesus responded, *"Yes, come"* —Matthew 14:29

So, what did Peter do?

He jumped!

"Peter went over the side of the boat and walked on the water toward Jesus." —Matthew 14:29

Think about it: before Jesus arrived at the scene, Peter's whole focus was on surviving the storm and staying in the boat. Gripped with fear and holding on for dear life, he and his friends just wanted to stay safe.

But when Peter saw Jesus walking on the water, faith arose. He wanted to get out of the boat and attempt something great. Peter was no longer focused on the danger of the storm and all the potential problems - he was now focused on Jesus and the possibilities ahead.

Peter jumped into the stormy sea and walked on the water.

There was no miracle for Peter in the boat. He had to step out of the boat for the miracle to be activated.

He had to dare to risk. He had to take a step of faith and jump.

As long as Peter kept his EYES ON JESUS, he could walk on the water. But he got scared. He looked at the storm, doubt rushed in, and it flooded his heart with fear once again. When Peter *"saw the strong wind and the waves, he was terrified and began to sink."* —Matthew 14:30

As Peter was slipping into the black stormy waters (remember it's around 3 am), he cried out, *"SAVE ME, LORD!"* —Matthew 14:30

As soon as he cried out for help, Jesus was there.

"Jesus immediately reached out and grabbed him. 'You have so little faith,' Jesus said. 'Why did you doubt me?'" —Matthew 14:31

You don't have to face your future alone. God wants to walk the journey with you. You can cry out to God to save you. You can invite Jesus into the boat of your life.

Jesus helped Peter walk back to the boat, and something miraculous happened...

"When they climbed back into the boat, the wind stopped. Then the disciples worshiped Him. 'You really are the Son of God!' they exclaimed. After they had crossed the lake, they landed at Gennesaret." — *Matthew 14:32-34*

Jesus calmed the storm and brought peace. He then took the disciples safely to the other side.

- IF JESUS IS WITH YOU IN YOUR BOAT, YOU WILL BE OKAY.
- DARE TO RISK FOR GOD.
- JUMP.
- FIX YOUR EYES ON JESUS.
- HE CAN CALM THE STORM.
- HE CAN TAKE YOU TO THE OTHER SIDE SAFELY.

Don't accept the false glass ceiling that you cannot accomplish something great. You have what it takes. You do not need to do it alone. God wants to take you on an adventure. It is time to dream. It is time to attempt great things with God at your side. It is time to dare to risk. It is time to position yourself to jump.

Are you ready? What are you waiting for?

Take that step.

5-4-3-2-1

J-U-M-P!

66

Jesus said, 'I have come that they may have life, and that they may have it more abundantly.'

John 10:10 NLT

Chapter 4

GOD CAN BRING DEAD DREAMS BACK TO LIFE!

Jesus Wants to Breathe New Life into You!

A few years ago, I shared a message of hope on the radio. In the middle of my message, I felt led to go in a different direction. I began to share a quote from Jesus as recorded in John 10:10.

Jesus said, *"The thief does not come except to steal, and to kill, and to destroy. I have come that they may have life, and that they may have it more abundantly." —John 10:10*

Little did I know, there was a lady who was alone at home. She was depressed and disillusioned with life. In fact, she had had enough. She felt like she could not carry on and had planned to end her life that night.

At the time, she was listening to another radio station. This lady shared that as she was about to end her life, her radio supernaturally changed stations. At this exact moment, I had shared the scripture on how the *"enemy had come to steal, kill, and to destroy,"* but how Jesus came to *"bring life, and life more abundantly."*

That night was a turning point in this precious lady's life. Instead of committing suicide, she shared how God miraculously changed her from the inside out.

That evening, God intervened, and instead of ending her life, she found the Savior. She found new life, abundant life!

God can do the same for you. He can take what seems dead and bring it back to life.

LIFE CAN BE TOUGH

We are living in crazy times. There is a lot of doom and gloom, but I believe God can make a way. He can bring light into the middle of your darkness. He can bring calm in the middle of your storm. He can bring new life to the lifeless.

No situation is so far gone that God cannot fix it.

Jesus brings new life. He can heal, deliver, and set free. Don't give up. Don't give in. Cry out to Jesus. He can do the impossible.

I want to encourage you to hold on, and I also want to pray for you. Although the enemy comes to steal, kill, and destroy, the good news is that Jesus came to bring life and life more abundantly.

Jesus said, *"Come to me, all you who are weary and burdened, and I will give you rest." —Matthew 11:28*

If you are overwhelmed or weighed down by the chaos of life, I want to encourage you to give your burdens to Jesus. You can rest in Him.

I believe that God can make a way. He can turn the tide. He is a miracle-working God.

JESUS BRINGS NEW LIFE

I want to look at the story of Lazarus, as found in John 11. Lazarus was a friend of Jesus. He had two sisters, Mary and Martha.

Now, Lazarus got extremely sick. Mary and Martha sent word to Jesus, asking Him to come heal their sick brother. After all, He was healing so many people. They knew He was able. But Jesus did not come right away, and Lazarus died.

Four days later, after Lazarus had already had his funeral and been buried, Jesus arrived. Jesus immediately went to meet with Mary and Martha. The sisters were terribly upset.

Mary told Jesus, *"If you had arrived earlier, our brother wouldn't have died."* Jesus' heart was broken. He was visibly upset and tried to reassure the sisters that everything would be okay. He went on and told them, *"Your brother will rise again." —John 11:23*

Jesus then said, *"'I am the resurrection and the life. Anyone who believes in me will live, even after dying.* ***Everyone who lives in me and believes in me will never ever die.'*** *And Jesus asked, 'Do you believe this?'" —John 11:25-26*

The sisters thought that Jesus was referring to the end of times when the dead would be resurrected, but Jesus had another idea. Jesus told the sisters that He wanted to see where Lazarus was buried. The sisters took Jesus to the grave site.

When Jesus arrived at the tomb, He instructed them to roll the tombstone away.

But Martha said, *"Jesus, my brother has been buried for four days already. His body is already decomposing. The stench will be terrible. You cannot go in there!"* —John 11:39

Then Jesus said, *"Did I not tell you that if you believe, you will see the glory of God?"* —John 11:40

So, at Jesus' instruction, they took the stone away and opened the grave.

Then Jesus looked up to heaven and prayed,

"Father, I thank you that you have heard me." — John 11:41

Then Jesus called in a loud voice, *"Lazarus, come out!"* —John 11:43

John 11:44 says, *"The dead man came out, his hands and feet wrapped with strips of linen, and a cloth around his face."*

Jesus raised Lazarus from the grave. His body was already rotting, but nothing is too far gone for Jesus.

Jesus not only brought Lazarus back to life. He also set him free from his sickness and bondage.

Jesus then said to them, *"Take off the grave clothes and let him go."*

Jesus delivered Lazarus from death and brought new life to him.

If Jesus can raise a dead man from the grave after four days, imagine what He can do for you.

Jesus is still the same God. He can do all things. He brings life and life more abundantly!

"Jesus Christ is the same yesterday, today, and forever." —Hebrews 13:8

Jesus is still the same today. He can still do what He did in Bible times in your life.

"Nothing is impossible with God." —Luke 1:37

God can fix anything!

"I am the Lord, the God of all the peoples of the world. Is anything too hard for me?" —Jeremiah 32:27

YOU MAY BE IN A HOPELESS AND IMPOSSIBLE SITUATION

Know this: **God can make a way**. After all, He raised a dead man from the grave!

He can resurrect your life.

Lazarus had been dead for four days, his body was already rotting and stinking, but Jesus brought hope to this hopeless situation.

Jesus offers you hope. He always brings hope to the hopeless.

DOES IT SEEM LIKE GOD HAS FORGOTTEN ABOUT YOU?

It may seem like God is too late. Jesus was four days too late for Lazarus, but He came in perfect time.

Maybe it seems like Jesus is four days too late for you. Maybe you have cried out to God for help. Perhaps you are sick, broken, or don't know what to do.

I need to encourage you: **Hold on! Wait on God! He sees you. He has not forgotten you.**

Maybe you have forgotten God. If so, come back to Him. You do not need to face life alone.

YOU MAY WANT TO GIVE UP

Maybe you cannot see any light at the end of the tunnel. You may want to throw in the towel.

I need to implore you: Don't give up! Don't give in! It is never too late for Jesus!

Jesus raised a dead man from the grave. He can make a way for you.

God can even *"make a road in the wilderness. And rivers in the desert." —Isaiah 43:19*

YOU MAY BE DOUBTING THAT GOD WILL COME THROUGH FOR YOU

God will come through in His perfect time. He is faithful.

Even when everything is down, you can rise! You can look to God. Expect the best!

Even when we are faithless, God remains faithful.

YOU MAY FEEL DEAD

You may be going through a crazy time. You may feel like your life is not worth living. Your heart may be beating, you may still be breathing, but you may feel dead on the inside.

Jesus can breathe new life into you.

Maybe you have lost your joy. Maybe you have lost your purpose and passion for life. You may have let go of your dreams.

You may be saying, "What's the point?"

Don't throw in the towel. Hold on! Don't quit. Don't

give up. Don't give in. **Jesus can resurrect your life. He can bring your dead dreams back to life.**

YOU MAY FEEL OPPRESSED

Jesus can remove that bondage. He can set you free and bring breakthrough.

When Lazarus came out of that grave, he was bound in his grave clothes. Jesus commanded that those clothes of bondage would be removed. He can release you from your bondage.

What has you in bondage? Whatever it is, it is no match for Jesus. He can break the chains that enslave you. **Jesus sets free!**

JESUS OFFERS YOU ETERNAL LIFE

Do you realize what Jesus did for you? On the cross, He paid the full price for our sins so that we could have complete forgiveness and abundant life.

There is more to life than just the here and now. God made you to live forever. One day, you will die, but your spirit will continue to live forever. In eternity, there is a heaven and a hell. Where will you spend your eternity?

Maybe you don't know Jesus as your Lord and Savior.

Jesus said, *"I am the resurrection and the life. **Anyone** who believes in me will live, even after dying. Everyone who lives in me and believes in me will never ever die." —John 11:25-26*

Invite Jesus into your life. He says, "ANYONE" who believes in me will have eternal life. **No one is excluded!** No matter who you are, where you are from, or what you have done, Jesus made it so clear that anyone can know God. You can come back to Him.

"Yet to all who did receive Him, to those who believed in his name, He gave the right to become children of God." —John 1:12

Jesus offers eternal life. Come back to Jesus. What are you waiting for?

SURRENDER YOUR LIFE AND BURDENS TO GOD

You may be in a situation that looks dead and buried.

Jesus brings hope. He brings abundant life. He can turn the tide. He can bring light into your darkness.

No matter what you are facing, Jesus can make a way.

All things are possible with God. It's not over until God says it's over.

You may feel like it's too late, but it's never too late for God. He is always on time. You may have cried out to Him and it may seem like Jesus doesn't care. He does!

Jesus arrived four days too late for Lazarus, but according to the Bible, He was in perfect time and showed his glory.

Remember, He is God. He sees the big picture.

He knows what is up. **Hold onto Jesus**.

You may feel dead with no hope. Jesus came to bring you life and life more abundantly.

God can. He can breathe new life into you. He can resurrect your life and dreams. He can calm your storm. He can restore. He offers new life. Eternal life. Abundant life.

Let us pray...

Dear Heavenly Father. I come to you, in the name of Jesus. I surrender my life to you, along with my sins and burdens. Lord Jesus thank you for paying the full price for my transgressions. Please forgive me. Please cleanse me. Please renew my life. I ask you to be my Lord and Savior.

Lord, you know exactly what is up. Please cause hope to arise. Father, I ask you to renew my mind. I ask you break the chains of bondage off my life. Lord, please bring breakthrough in my life. I ask you to deliver me and set me free. Please pour out your supernatural favor and bring complete restoration to my life. May your peace flow like a mighty river in my heart.

Holy Spirit, please breathe new life into me. Fan into flames a new passion in my heart for you. Thank you that I am forgiven, renewed, revived, and restored. Thank you for your resurrection power working in me. Thank you for life and life more abundantly.

I pray this in Jesus' name, Amen.

Now lift your hands to heaven and receive your freedom. Receive God's gift of abundant life. May your life never be the same again.

If you have prayed this prayer, please <u>let us know</u>. We would love to pray for you and send you some incredible resources to help you in your journey with God.

JESUS CAME TO BRING YOU LIFE AND LIFE MORE ABUNDANTLY

Hold onto God. Put your faith in Jesus Christ.

Remember that no situation is too far gone for Jesus. Nothing is too late for Jesus.

He not only raised a dead man from the grave, but He healed and delivered him from his bondage.

JESUS BRINGS DEAD THINGS BACK TO LIFE.

JESUS BRINGS NEW LIFE.

JESUS BRINGS HOPE.

HE LOVES TO HEAL AND DELIVER.

JESUS BRINGS BREAKTHROUGH.

HE SETS FREE.

"Therefore, if the Son makes you free, you shall be free indeed." —John 8:36

Don't give up. Don't give in. Hold on! Cry out to Jesus. He can do the impossible.

It is time to start afresh and dream again. God is bringing dead things back to life.

DARE TO DREAM

66

Lord, I want to see.

Mark 10:52

Chapter 5

FRESH VISION

God Can Bring the Walls Down.

S ometimes, we are blinded from the opportunities that are right in front of us. This can be caused by walls of obstruction beyond our control.

We need fresh vision.

Jesus said, *"The thief does not come except to steal, and to kill, and to destroy. **I have come that they may have life, and that they may have it more abundantly.**"* —John 10:10

Jesus told us clearly that the enemy comes to...

- Kill
- Steal
- Destroy

Thank God that Jesus didn't stop there! He went on and told us the good news.

Jesus said that He *"came to bring life and life more abundantly."*

The enemy's purpose is to bring destruction and chaos. He comes to cause division, strife, and pain. The biggest battle you face is in your mind, where the enemy wants to steal your dreams and blind your vision.

Life can be challenging. You might be facing many difficulties. But I want to encourage you to put your hope in God. Keep a good attitude. Smile! Look on the bright side of life. Keep dreaming. Rekindle your vision.

No matter what you are facing, there is hope. God can turn your mourning into dancing. He can turn the tide. He can bring light into your dark place.

You do not need to face life alone. God wants to walk the journey with you.

WALLS OF OBSTRUCTION

You may have huge obstructions in your way that are making it difficult to have vision. Walls of oppression may surround your life.

Joshua 6 tells the story of the City of Jericho. This city had large, impenetrable walls. The walls were so thick that chariots could race on top. Maybe you feel like you have Jericho walls of bondage keeping you imprisoned and enslaved.

God brought the walls of Jericho down. He can also bring the walls of depression, oppression, and bondage down in your life.

Nothing is too difficult for God.

If you have lost your vision and let go of your hopes and dreams, call on Jesus. He can bring down the walls that are blocking your vision. He is the gateway of hope. He is the doorway to abundant life.

THE BLIND BEGGAR

Many years after God had brought down the walls of Jericho, Jesus came to this city.

In this city, Jesus met a blind beggar named Bartimaeus. This guy had no hope. He had no vision and nothing to look forward to. His future was dark.

But when Bartimaeus heard that Jesus was in town, a spark of hope flooded his heart. Suddenly, he thought, "I've heard of this Jesus. I've heard the stories of how He does miracles. Maybe He can do a miracle for me."

Bartimaeus started crying out, "Jesus, Son of David, have mercy on me!"

He got desperate. He did his best to get Jesus' attention. The crowd tried to shut Bartimaeus up, but he just shouted louder, *"Jesus, have mercy on me!"* — *Mark 10:48*

Jesus called for Bartimaeus to be brought to Him.

When this blind beggar approached Jesus, Jesus asked Bartimaeus, **"What do you want Me to do for you?"** —*Mark 10:51*

He answered Jesus, *"**Lord, I want to see**."*

Then Jesus told him, *"'Go your way; your faith has made you well.' And **immediately he received his sight and followed Jesus** on the road." —Mark 10:52*

Jesus brought down the walls of darkness. He brought Bartimaeus new life. Not only did Jesus open his blind eyes, but He also gave Bartimaeus new hope and a new vision.

Think of it: Bartimaeus had nothing to aspire to as a beggar. He had no plans or dreams. He thought he had no hope for the future. But when Jesus brought down the walls of blindness, Bartimaeus could not only see the beauty of God's creation and his family (who he had never seen before!), but he also had a new vision for the future.

Bartimaeus could now leave his old life as a beggar. He could dare to dream. He had a fresh vision for the future. He could move forward.

NEW VISION

God can give you a new vision.

The enemy may have stolen your vision. Your circumstances may have been obstacles that have stopped you from dreaming. Walls of oppression may have held you back from dreaming of a brighter future.

It is not how you start the journey but how you end it that counts.

Maybe you need to regain your vision. You may need to find your way.

Jesus is the way maker. Draw near to Him. Cry out to Him, like Bartimaeus did. Come boldly to God's throne of grace. God can bring the walls down. He can take what the enemy meant for evil and turn it around for good.

DARE TO DREAM

66

*The Lord was with Joseph,
so he succeeded in
everything he did.*

Genesis 39:2

Chapter 6

SETBACKS AND COMEBACKS

God Can Take Your Setback
and Turn it into a Comeback!

Y ou may have had a setback in your life. Maybe you've chased a dream but failed and feel discouraged. I have a simple message for you: No matter what you are facing or where you find yourself, I need you to know that God can take your **mess** and turn it into a **message**! God can take your **test** and turn it into a **testimony**.

God can take your **setback** and turn it into a **comeback**.

There is an incredible story in the Bible where a man named Joseph had a series of setbacks. Not only was God with him in his desperate situation, but God delivered him.

JOSEPH

Joseph was born when his father, Jacob, was very old. He was his dad's favorite child. His dad bought him an incredible multi-colored coat that made him stand out. This made his brothers jealous of him.

To make matters worse, Joseph had two dreams where he saw his brothers bowing down to him. He shared how *"The sun, moon, and eleven stars bowed low before me!" —Genesis 37:9*

Instead of keeping this dream to himself, he shared it with his brothers, which just infuriated them more. So much so that his older brothers wanted to kill him!

The time came when Joseph was sent to check on his brothers who were out in the wilderness looking after the family flocks. The brothers discussed how this was an opportunity to get rid of Joseph once and for all. They planned to kill him, but they ended up throwing him in a pit with the plan of leaving him there to die.

But a group of traders was passing by on their way to Egypt, and the brothers decided to sell Joseph to them.

To cover their crime, the brothers "killed a young goat and dipped Joseph's robe in its blood. They sent the beautiful robe to their father with this message: *"Look at what we found. Doesn't this robe belong to your son?" —Genesis 37:31-32*

They implied that a wild animal must have eaten him, leaving just his blood-stained robe that was torn into pieces.

CRUSHED DREAMS

Joseph had a dream. He felt that God had a special plan for his life. Still, he ended up getting thrown into a pit by his own brothers, barely surviving a planned murder, and being sold into slavery. It looked like he would have nothing to look forward to except for a life of misery and pain under the oppression of slavery, but **God wasn't finished with this young man!**

When the traders *"arrived in Egypt,"* they ended up selling *"Joseph to Potiphar, an officer of Pharaoh, the king of Egypt. Potiphar was captain of the palace guard." —Genesis 37:36*

Of all the people Joseph could have been sold to, he ended up in the best place possible, living in the palace as a servant to the second most influential person in the whole of Egypt.

*"**The Lord was with Joseph, so he succeeded in everything he did** as he served in the home of his Egyptian master." —Genesis 39:2 NLT*

God turned his **setback** into a great **comeback**!

In fact, we are told, *"Potiphar noticed this and realized that **the Lord was with Joseph, giving him success in everything he did**. This pleased Potiphar, so he soon made Joseph his personal attendant. He **put him in charge** of his entire household and everything he owned. From the day Joseph was put in charge of his master's household and property, **the Lord began to bless Potiphar's household for Joseph's sake**. All his household affairs ran smoothly, and his crops and livestock flourished." —Genesis 39:3-5*

PIT TO PALACE

Joseph went from the **pit** to the **palace**.

In the palace, Joseph became Potiphar's managing director, taking over the *"complete administrative responsibility over everything he owned"* and *"with Joseph there, he didn't worry about a thing." —Genesis 39:6*

Everything was going well for Joseph. He was also *"a very handsome and well-built young man." —Genesis 39:6*

And this led to a huge **setback**. Potiphar's wife took a fancy to Joseph and tried to woo him into having an affair with her.

We are told, *"She kept putting pressure on Joseph day after day, but he refused to sleep with her, and he kept out of her way as much as possible. One day, however, no one else was around when he went in to do his work. She came and grabbed him by his cloak, demanding, 'Come on, sleep with me!' Joseph tore himself away, but he left his cloak in her hand as he ran from the house." —Genesis 39:10-12*

She fabricated a story about how Joseph had tried to take advantage of her. She made up a story saying, *"He came into my room to rape me but I screamed."* And when *"he heard me scream, he ran outside and got away, but he left his cloak behind with me." — Genesis 39:14-15*

Joseph's cloak was used as "evidence" against him. We are told that *"Potiphar was furious when he heard his wife's story about how Joseph had treated her. So*

he took Joseph and threw him into the prison where the king's prisoners were held, and there he remained."
—Genesis 39:19-20

PALACE TO PRISON

From living in the palace and holding a position of influence, Joseph was falsely accused and ended up in prison. This second huge **setback** in Joseph's life could have left him forever defeated. But God was with him, and when God is with you, all will work out okay.

*"**But the Lord was with Joseph in the prison and showed him His faithful love**. And the Lord made Joseph a **favorite** with the prison warden. Before long, the warden **put Joseph in charge** of all the other prisoners and over everything that happened in the prison. The warden had no more worries because Joseph took care of everything. **The Lord was with him and caused everything he did to succeed**." —Genesis 39:21-23*

Now a while later, Pharaoh's chief cupbearer and chief baker offended their royal master, and they ended up in the same prison where Joseph was. And one night both men had a troubling dream.

God had given Joseph the ability to interpret dreams. After the cupbearer shared his dream with Joseph, he told him, *"Within three days Pharaoh will lift you up and restore you to your position as his chief cupbearer." —Genesis 40:13*

Joseph asked the cupbearer, *"And please*

remember me and do me a favor when things go well for you. Mention me to Pharaoh, so he might let me out of this place." —Genesis 40:14

When the chief baker saw that Joseph had given the first dream such a positive interpretation, he asked Joseph to interpret his dream too. Unfortunately, the chief baker's dream was bad news. Joseph shared that *"Three days from now Pharaoh will lift you up and impale your body on a pole. Then birds will come and peck away at your flesh." —Genesis 40:19*

And guess what happened...

We are told that *"Pharaoh's birthday came three days later, and he prepared a banquet for all his officials and staff. He summoned his chief cupbearer and chief baker to join the other officials." —Genesis 40:20*

"He then restored the chief cupbearer to his former position, so he could again hand Pharaoh his cup. But Pharaoh impaled the chief baker, just as Joseph had predicted when he interpreted his dream." —Genesis 40:21-22

We are also told that *"Pharaoh's chief cupbearer, however, forgot all about Joseph, never giving him another thought." —Genesis 40:23*

Another two years passed. Joseph is **still in prison**.

One night Pharaoh had two dreams that deeply disturbed him. One about cows and another about grain. He called for all the magicians and wise men of Egypt. When Pharaoh told them his dreams, not one of them could tell him what they meant.

This is when the king's chief cupbearer remembered Joseph. He told Pharaoh, *"Some time ago, you were angry with the chief baker and me, and you imprisoned us in the palace of the captain of the guard. One night the chief baker and I each had a dream, and each dream had its own meaning. There was a young Hebrew man with us in the prison who was a slave of the captain of the guard. We told him our dreams, and he told us what each of our dreams meant. And everything happened just as he had predicted. I was restored to my position as cupbearer, and the chief baker was executed and impaled on a pole."* —*Genesis 41:11-13*

PRISON TO POWER

Pharaoh wasted no time. He called for Joseph at once, and he was quickly brought from the prison.

"Then Pharaoh said to Joseph, 'I had a dream last night, and no one here can tell me what it means. But I have heard that when you hear about a dream you can interpret it.' 'It is beyond my power to do this,' Joseph replied. 'But God can tell you what it means and set you at ease.' So Pharaoh told Joseph his dream." —*Genesis 41:15-17*

God immediately gave Joseph the ability to interpret Pharaoh's dreams.

"Joseph responded, 'Both of Pharaoh's dreams mean the same thing. God is telling Pharaoh in advance what he is about to do. The seven healthy cows and the seven healthy heads of grain both

represent seven years of prosperity. The seven thin, scrawny cows that came up later and the seven thin heads of grain, withered by the east wind, represent seven years of famine. This will happen just as I have described it, for God has revealed to Pharaoh in advance what he is about to do. The next seven years will be a period of great prosperity throughout the land of Egypt. But afterward, there will be seven years of famine so great that all the prosperity will be forgotten in Egypt. Famine will destroy the land.'" — *Genesis 41:25-30*

Joseph shared that the dream was a warning of what would soon happen. He shared how there would be seven prosperous years followed by a devastating drought for seven years, and that unless drastic measures were put in place without delay, Egypt would not survive.

Joseph then gave Pharaoh a **strategic plan** he could apply to get through this tough period. It involved finding an intelligent and wise man who could be put in charge of the entire land of Egypt with a plan to collect one fifth of all the crops during the seven good years.

The plan also involved appointing supervisors and ensuring that 20% of all crops were stored away and well-guarded with a system to ensure food could be distributed to the needy during the period of severe famine. Joseph shared that without putting the right measures in place that *"famine will destroy the land."* —*Genesis 41:36*

"Joseph's suggestions were well received by Pharaoh and his officials. So Pharaoh asked his officials, 'Can we find anyone else like this man so obviously filled with the spirit of God?'" —Genesis 41:37-38

Without any further thought, "Pharaoh said to Joseph, '**Since God has revealed the meaning of the dreams to you, clearly no one else is as intelligent or wise as you are**. You will be in charge of my court, and all my people will take orders from you. Only I, sitting on my throne, will have a rank higher than yours.' Pharaoh said to Joseph, '**I hereby put you in charge of the entire land of Egypt.**'" —Genesis 41:39-41

Pharaoh put Joseph in charge of **the entire land of Egypt**. He literally went from **zero to hero** in a few hours. He came straight from the pit of prison to the position of second in command of the entire country. And Pharaoh told Joseph, going forward, "No one will lift a hand or foot in the entire land of Egypt without your approval." —Genesis 41:44

God took Joseph from prison back to the palace. **God can do the same in your life.** You may have had a **setback**, but God can turn it into the greatest **comeback** ever. He can take your **mess** and turn it into a **message**. He can take your **test** and turn it into a **testimony**.

SEVEN YEARS OF PROSPERITY

"As predicted, for seven years the land produced bumper crops. During those years, Joseph gathered *all the crops grown in Egypt and stored the grain from the surrounding fields in the cities. He piled up huge amounts of grain like sand on the seashore. Finally, he stopped keeping records because there was too much to measure." —Genesis 41:47-49*

FAVOR IN THE MIDDLE OF FAMINE

After the seven years of plenty and stockpiling provisions, the dreaded famine hit the land just as God had shown Joseph.

"Then the seven years of famine began, just as Joseph had predicted. The famine also struck all the surrounding countries, but throughout Egypt there was plenty of food. Eventually, however, the famine spread throughout the land of Egypt as well. And when the people cried out to Pharaoh for food, he told them, 'Go to Joseph, and do whatever he tells you.' So with severe famine everywhere, Joseph opened up the storehouses and distributed grain to the Egyptians, for the famine was severe throughout the land of Egypt. And people from all around came to Egypt to buy grain from Joseph because the famine was severe throughout the world." —Genesis 41:54-57

God saved an entire nation because of Joseph. They all would have died of starvation if Joseph had not been able to interpret the dream and if he didn't have the God-given solution to their problem. With **God's supernatural empowerment and wisdom**, Joseph was able to implement a workable strategy to safeguard Egypt.

No matter where you are today, keep your chin up. Stay obedient. Keep your eyes on Jesus. Stay connected to God. In due course, God will lift you up. **Not only can God take you from prison to the palace, but He can also use you to change your world!**

The famine was so severe that it even affected the surrounding nations. Joseph's family was living in Canaan. They were starving and traveled to Egypt to try to get supplies.

Little would they know that their young brother – the one they had planned to kill and ended up selling into slavery – would be the one to save them!

"So Jacob's sons arrived in Egypt along with others to buy food, for the famine was in Canaan as well. Since Joseph was governor of all Egypt and in charge of selling grain to all the people, it was to him that his brothers came. When they arrived, they bowed before him with their faces to the ground." —Genesis 42:5-6)

We are told that *"Although Joseph recognized his brothers, they didn't recognize him. And he remembered the dreams he'd had about them many years before." —Genesis 42:8-9*

His **childhood dream** of his brothers bowing before him had come to pass.

When his brothers arrived, Joseph could have had them arrested. After all, they planned to **murder him and sold him into slavery**. But Joseph didn't get bitter. **He forgave his brothers.**

WATCH OUT FOR BITTERNESS

Keep your heart pure. **Forgive.** This can be the one blockage to your freedom that can prevent God from turning your setback into a comeback.

Joseph then, through a series of events and much to his brother's surprise, revealed his identity to them.

Joseph showed great **mercy** to his brothers. He forgave them.

"'Please, come closer,' he said to them. So they came closer. And he said again, 'I am Joseph, your brother, whom you sold into slavery in Egypt. But don't be upset, and don't be angry with yourselves for selling me to this place. It was God who sent me here ahead of you to preserve your lives.'" —Genesis 45:4-5

Joseph then shared with his brothers how God had revealed to him that *"this famine that has ravaged the land for two years will last five more years, and there will be neither plowing nor harvesting. God has sent me ahead of you to keep you and your families alive and to preserve many survivors. **So, it was God who sent me here, not you!** And he is the one who made me an adviser to Pharaoh—the manager of his entire palace and the governor of all Egypt. He then told his brothers, 'Now hurry back to my father and tell him, 'This is what your son Joseph says: God has made me master over all the land of Egypt. So come down to me immediately! You can live in the region of Goshen, where you can be near me with all your children and grandchildren, your flocks and herds, and everything* *you own. I will take care of you there, for there are still five years of famine ahead of us. Otherwise you, your household, and all your animals will starve.'"* — *Genesis 45:6-11*

What Joseph's brothers had meant for **evil**, God turned around for **good**. God can turn it around!

Joseph faced many **setbacks**, but God turned these setbacks into great **comebacks** that not only changed his life and saved his family, but ensured that a whole nation survived.

IT IS TIME FOR A COMEBACK!

Joseph literally went from zero to hero.

Today no matter what you are facing or where you find yourself, I need you to know that...

- **God can take your mess and turn it into a message.**
- **God can take your test and turn it into a testimony.**
- **God can take your setback and turn it into a comeback.**

Are you prepared to surrender your life, along with your setbacks to God? Just like God was with Joseph, so He wants to do life with you.

He is with you in your pit. He is with you in your prison. He can pour out His favor and success on you, even in the middle of your mess.

God can bring you out. God can turn your **setback** into a great **comeback**! All you need to do is surrender your life and setbacks to God.

Jesus told us that in this world we will face storms, trials, and troubles but He also told us to **take heart**.

Why?

Because **He has overcome the world**!

Jesus said, *"I have told you these things, so that in me you may have peace. In this world you will have trouble. But take heart! I have overcome the world."* — *John 16:33 NIV*

Jesus has all power and authority. He can do all things. He can turn the tide. He can calm your storm. He can bring light into your darkness. He can turn your setback into the greatest comeback of all time.

God is with you in your dark valleys.

"Even though I walk through the darkest valley, I will fear no evil, for you are with me; your rod and your staff, they comfort me." —Psalms 23:4 NIV

God will see you through. He will help you survive in the middle of your setback. He will bring you through.

God says, ***"When you pass through the waters, I will be with you; and when you pass through the rivers, they will not sweep over you. When you walk through the fire, you will not be burned; the flames will not set you ablaze." —Isaiah 43:2***

Why?

For God is your Savior.

He wants to lift you up! He wants you to be fruitful and thrive in your comeback!

"I am the vine; you are the branches. If you remain

in me and I in you, you will bear much fruit; apart from me you can do nothing." —John 15:5 NIV

You need to be connected to Jesus. You need to remain close to God.

If you have fallen away from God, call on Jesus. If you are in the middle of a setback, even if it is due to your own mistakes, errors, and evil ways, return to God.

"For God so loved the world that He gave his one and only Son, that whoever believes in Him shall not perish but have eternal life." —John 3:16 NIV

Do you know that the name "Jesus" means Savior? He came to save you.

We are told, ***"Everyone who calls on the name of the Lord will be saved."*** *—Romans 10:13 NIV*

And this includes you.

HAVE YOU LOST YOUR WAY?

If you have drifted from God or lost your way, it is time to come back to God.

Return to God.

Are you stuck in a pit that you just cannot get out of?

Your pit may be an addiction, a financial debt, or a bondage you are stuck in. Jesus has a long extendable arm of love. He can reach into your pit, into the mud, lift you up and set you back on a solid foundation.

Are you in some type of prison?

Maybe you are not physically locked away, but you

may be a prisoner in your mind, bound to anxiety, depression, or even limiting beliefs. God can break the chains. He can unlock your prison door. He can break you out of your oppression. Maybe sin has you enslaved. Jesus can set you free.

PUT JESUS AT THE CENTER

If you have placed your faith in Jesus, you can rest assured that He is with you, even in your most trying situation...

Jesus said, *"And be sure of this:* **I am with you always, even to the end of the age."** *—Matthew 28:20 NLT*

If you have placed your trust in Jesus, you can be assured that nothing will ever separate you from his love...

"And I am convinced that nothing can ever separate us from God's love. Neither death nor life, neither angels nor demons, neither our fears for today nor our worries about tomorrow—not even the powers of hell can separate us from God's love." —Romans 8:38 NLT

If Jesus is with you, He will be your strength...

"For I can do everything through Christ who gives me strength." —Philippians 4:13 NLT

If you love Jesus, He will work it all out for the good.

"And we know that God causes everything to work together for the good of those who love God and are called according to his purpose for them." —Romans 8:28 NLT

If Jesus is at the center of your life, you will get through this...

"And my God will meet all your needs according to the riches of his glory in Christ Jesus." —*Philippians 4:19 NIV*

If Jesus is your Lord and Savior, you will find victory...

"No, despite all these things, overwhelming victory is ours through Christ, who loved us." —*Romans 8:37 NLT*

God can take you out of the pit and place you in the palace.

God can deliver you from the prison you may find yourself in and He can elevate you to a position of power.

It is not how you start the race that matters. It is how you finish!

God can bring **light** into your **darkness**.

God can turn your **mourning** into **dancing**.

God can lift you up out of the **sinking sand** and place you on a **solid rock**.

God can **restore** what the locust has devoured.

God can place **joy** back in your heart and give you a new song to sing.

God can **fix** what is broken.

God can turn your upside-down life **the right way around**.

God can **heal**, **deliver**, and **set you free**.

God can turn your **famine** into a **feast**.

God can take your stunted desolate life and make it **fruitful** and **flourishing**.

Surrender your life to Jesus. Give Him your burdens. Give Him your setbacks.

Hand the reigns of your life over to Jesus. Make Jesus the center.

God can turn your setback into the greatest comeback of all time!

"See, I am doing a new thing. Now it springs up; do you not perceive it? I am making a way in the wilderness and streams in the wasteland." —Isaiah 43:19

DARE TO DREAM

66

***Whatever you do,
work at it with all your heart,
as working for the Lord,
not for human masters.***

Colossians 3:23

Chapter 7

EXTRAORDINARY

You Don't Have to Be Ordinary.
You Can Change.

Most people have had a big dream at one stage or another, a dream that excited them and spurred them on with the hope of accomplishing greatness.

But unfortunately, the dream stealer knocks them down, and that one hard knock takes them off course. At this stage most throw in the towel and let go of their dreams. It breaks my heart to see people who once had such passion and purpose give up on their hopes and aspirations and settle for mediocrity.

Unfortunately, the average person gives up far too quickly and takes the easy road. Many, out of fear of failure, end up just going through the motions, floating through life without achieving their dreams.

If this sums up your life, you probably feel discouraged and frustrated. You may have lost your joy and passion for life.

I know many who are battling through life. In the current economic climate, I know life can be tough. So many are left cash-strapped, stressed out, and debt-ridden, with only shattered dreams, no vision, and little to look forward to in life. Many are living in survival mode, battling to keep their head above water.

Have you just accepted your current circumstances as your lot in life? If this is where you find yourself, I have to encourage you to lift the lid and dream again.

You don't have to live like this. You can get back up. You can begin again.

Don't settle for average. The average person has no meaningful goals or dreams.

I have some good news for you. If you are sick and tired of just following the crowd with nothing to look forward to, you can make a CHANGE. You don't have to be ordinary. You can set yourself up to be EXTRAORDINARY by making a few simple changes to your attitude.

To be extraordinary is to be remarkable, exceptional, and above average.

Choose to be a person of excellence.

"Whatever you do, work at it with all your heart, as working for the Lord, not for human masters." — Colossians 3:23

I do not know where you are standing today or what you have been through, but I do believe that with a few simple changes and with God's help, you can set yourself up not just to have an ordinary future but one that is EXTRAORDINARY, filled with purpose and with a new lease on life.

Don't settle for less than what you are meant to be. God made you, and He doesn't make junk. He knit you together in your mother's womb. He planted a dream in your heart, a God-ordained destiny for you to fulfill. God has given you unique talents and abilities. Find out what they are and press on until you reach your potential.

It is not how you start the race but how you end it that counts.

When you get knocked down, get up again. Shake off the dust and get going.

You can move from surviving to thriving. You can attempt great things with God.

You can start afresh. It may take some time to get back on your feet and turn your life around, but you can restart your engine.

It starts with a choice. Draw a line in the sand. Lift your head. Dare to dream once again. Set some goals and ask God to help you. God can take you out of the valley of despair and launch you into a fruitful season.

Albert Einstein said, *"The definition of insanity is doing the same thing the same way, expecting different results."*

You cannot do the same thing the same way and expect a different result. Something needs to change!

Are you prepared to change?

THE VECTOR PRINCIPLE

Have you heard of the vector principle?

When an airplane takes off, it takes a straight path toward its destination. It doesn't get to a stop street and then turn left. It sets off towards its destination and then only makes tiny changes occasionally to stay on course. If an airplane is on a long flight and is just one degree off, it could be the difference between landing in France or London!

If you make small changes regularly, you will see a massive change over the long term.

TINY CHOICES TODAY CAN HAVE A HUGE IMPACT TOMORROW

Life is full of choices, and the decisions you make today have a significant impact on your future.

Make good choices. They usually lead to good results, while bad choices lead to bad ones.

Our choices become our habits, and unless we are intentional with our goals and plans, things usually don't work out well.

If I eat one doughnut, it won't make much of a difference, but eating five doughnuts each day will make me fat and unhealthy over time. While the impact of me eating five doughnuts a day will not show in the first week, the result of my eating will be evident for all to see over time.

Where are you currently?

If you keep doing what you are currently doing, where will you be in 10 years from now?

Craig Groeschel said, *"The decisions you make today will determine the stories we tell about our lives tomorrow. Every day, all day, we make one decision after another. These choices keep accumulating, each one woven together into the rest, forming the tapestry that is our life story."*

You are one choice away from changing your life.

What dreams have you let go of? What needs to change? What are the non-negotiables?

What do you need to do differently? Do you need to reorganize your priorities?

HOW DO YOU EAT AN ELEPHANT?

Often, trying to achieve a BIG dream can seem like an impossible task.

Whether you want to lose a ton of weight, squash a mountain of debt, or build up a huge wealth portfolio, it can seem impossible, as if it is out of reach.

Dave Ramsey said, *"Don't try to tackle too much at once. Break your goals down into smaller pieces that you reach one action at a time."*

Brian Tracy said, *"Any goal can be achieved if you break it down into small enough parts."*

There is an old saying: *"How do you eat an elephant?"*

The answer is: *"In bite-size chunks!"*

It would help if you broke down your BIG dreams into easy-to-achieve bite-size chunks.

What is your ELEPHANT?

How can you break it down into BITE-SIZE CHUNKS?

You may need to get advice from your health professional, banker, or financial advisor. You may need to plan and look at your ELEPHANT from various angles. It would be best if you came up with a solution to achieving your goal in the easiest way possible.

Develop a realistic plan. Break it down into a series of smaller, easy-to-follow steps that can become stepping stones to take you from where you are to where you want to be.

Set up a timeframe.

The easier your plan is to achieve, the greater your chance of following through.

If this sums up your life, and if you want to change, then I am going to ask you to do three things...

STOP!

Assess your current situation. Don't bury your head in the sand and pretend that you do not have a problem. Face your fears and decide to start over. Choose to lift the lid. Invite God to be part of your journey.

"Trust in the LORD with all your heart and lean not on your own understanding; in all your ways submit to Him, and He will make your paths straight."—Psalm 3:5-6

FACE YOUR FEARS

I want to ask you to do something scary:

Face your fears!

Look that giant of a problem in the eye and say, "Enough is enough."

Commit your plans and your life to God. If you have messed up, face this and ask God to forgive you. Jesus already paid the price for you, so surrender your past mistakes to Him.

BE PREPARED TO CHANGE

You can exchange your ordinary for the extraordinary. If your current situation is not working, you need to do something differently, or you will never see a positive change.

Dave Ramsey said, *"If you want something you have never had, you'll need to do something you've never done!"*

Choose today to give up on your old ways of doing things that are not working. You may need to make a few changes.

Why don't you try to set up a new strategy that can lead you to success?

I encourage you to get your priorities in order.

I encourage you to ask yourself three questions...

Where am I at present?

Be honest with yourself. What is working?

What is not? Analyze how things are going.

Where would I like to be?

Dare to dream again. Set some new goals.

How could I get there?

Set up a plan and a new strategy to move forward.

You can't do the same thing the same way and expect a different result. Something needs to change! If you want something you have never had, you must do something you've never done.

As John Maxwell says, *"If you change your attitude, you can change your altitude."*

You may have failed, but you can fail forward. You Let go of the ordinary. Choose to be extraordinary.

PART TWO

THE PRACTICE

66

For I am about to do something new.
See, I have already begun!
Do you not see it?
I will make a pathway
through the wilderness.
I will create rivers
in the dry wasteland.

Isaiah 43:19

Chapter 8

PICTURE. PLAN. PROCESS.

Your Dreams Can Drive You to Your Destiny
or to a Dead End.

It is important to dream. Dreams inspire. Dreams cause our hearts to beat a little faster. Dreams can revive and reignite purpose and passion in our hearts.

DREAMS BRING HOPE AND A VISION FOR THE FUTURE

A dream for your future can spark hope, spur you on to greatness, and give you a fresh lease on life.

Life can be mundane and pointless if you don't have a dream for the future.

IF A DREAM DOESN'T COME TRUE IT CAN LEAD TO DREAD AND LEAVE YOU DEFEATED

If you have a dream in your heart that doesn't materialize, it can leave you feeling frustrated, devastated, and hopeless!

King Solomon summed it up well when he said, **"Hope deferred makes the heart sick, but a dream fulfilled is a tree of life."** —Proverbs 13:12 NLT

According to King Solomon, it leads to hopelessness when you don't achieve your dreams. This, in turn, may lower your future expectations or even stop you from dreaming to avoid disappointment.

HAVING A DREAM IS NOT ENOUGH

Most people who have dreams don't end up fulfilling them because they miss the essential steps required to turn a dream into reality.

In the following few chapters, I want to encourage you to dare to dream and aim high.

I also want to give the key missing steps that you can apply to help you achieve your dreams. And when you do achieve your dreams, it leads to life and joy.

THERE IS A PROCESS YOU CAN FOLLOW TO HELP YOU ACHIEVE YOUR DREAMS.

To achieve your dreams, you need a clear...

- PICTURE
- PLAN
- PROCESS

A CLEAR PICTURE OF YOUR DREAM AND VISION

God made you one of a kind. No one is quite like you. He made you unique, with a special destiny to fulfill. God has planted a dream inside of you that is yours alone to achieve. Only you can birth it.

God has gifted you with special abilities that no one else has. So, you don't have to follow the crowd.

Be the best YOU that God made YOU to be. God has put the potential on the inside of you.

DREAM BIG

A friend once told me something profound about living your dreams out.

He said, *"Find something you love doing that you are prepared to do for free. Then get so good at it that people will pay you for it."*

This was his definition of **living your dream**. I have encouraged my children to follow this, and I aspire to do this, too.

What are your dreams for the future? What are you passionate about? What drives you? What is your purpose? Have you found your place in this world? What are you good at? What do you enjoy doing? What inspires you? What excites you?

The answers to these questions often reveal your dreams.

BIG PICTURE

Go after your dreams. Your dreams will give you a big-picture view of your aspirations for the future.

If your dream was building a house, you would start by seeing the image of the finished product in your head. However, to see your dream become a reality, you need to act on the dream.

You need to picture your dream in your head and heart before it can become a reality. We will go deeper into this in the next chapter!

Many have big dreams but never see them come to fruition because it requires work to move the dream from a picture in your mind to becoming real. It is, therefore, essential to build on your dreams, and that's where vision comes in...

SKETCH YOUR VISION

Without a dream, you have nothing to look forward to, and a dream without a working solution will leave you unfulfilled and frustrated. It is so important to take the dream in your heart and bring it to life. This starts with a vision.

If your dream is the image in your head and heart, you now need the vision to "visualize it." This will help give you a clear outline of what is required to accomplish your dream.

If your dream were building a house, your vision would be the process of making a rough sketch. This involves taking your dream in your head and placing an image on paper of what you want to see materialize.

Once you see it, you can begin the work needed to achieve it.

"Where there is no vision, the people perish." — Proverbs 29:18

A vision will help you construct a well-defined mental image of how you can achieve your dreams. As you create a rough sketch, your dream will start to take shape. However, the sketch now needs to become a plan to accomplish your dream.

A CLEAR PLAN

Your plan is the blueprint of what will be needed to make your dream a reality.

If you were building a house, you would start with the dream. You then need to create a vision. Once you have a rough sketch, you now need to get the architect to construct a plan of what the final picture looks like. This includes the exact dimensions required and a finished blueprint of what is needed to turn your dream home into a real home.

MAP

Your plan is the map to get from where you are to where you want to be. It is the plan of how to take your dream and turn it into a reality.

Once you construct a workable plan, you will be on your way to achieving your dream.

"Good planning and hard work lead to prosperity, but hasty shortcuts lead to poverty." —Proverbs 21:5)

Hasty shortcuts lead to failure, but if you devise a good plan and work at it, you can turn your dreams into reality. Working on a good plan and being disciplined enough to follow through will lead to a successful outcome.

All you now need to do is follow through on the plan, and you will bring your dream to reality. This is where a strategy is required.

A CLEAR PROCESS

Having a process is all about breaking your plan down into smaller stepping stones. Your strategy is taking your plan and setting up an easy-to-follow step-by-step process to help you fulfill your dream.

If you were building a house, the strategy would be the step-by-step process to turn the dream home into a reality. This would involve calculating the cost and working out what is needed. It would start with the plot, the blueprint, and the process. First, you would hire the right builder, position the home, build a solid foundation, and then construct the walls and, eventually, the roof. By following the step-by-step process, you will end up with your dream becoming a reality.

"By wisdom a house is built, and through understanding it is established; through knowledge its rooms are filled with rare and beautiful treasures." — Proverbs 24:3-4

Your strategy is simply breaking down your plan into smaller stepping stones that you can easily follow, step-by-step, to bring your dream to fruition.

DON'T GIVE UP.
DON'T GIVE IN.
DON'T DREAD.

Let go of the frustrations and disillusions.
HAVE A CLEAR PICTURE, PLAN AND PROCESS.

Dare to dream. Set up the map. Simplify the strategy.

In the following few chapters, I will give you the practical steps needed to articulate your dream and turn it into reality.

66

Good planning and hard work
lead to prosperity,
but hasty shortcuts
lead to poverty.

Proverbs 21:5

Chapter 9

GOOD PLANNING
LEADS TO SUCCESS

Plan well. Work at your plan. Follow through.

I want to share one of my favorite bedrock scriptures with you on how to be successful at anything you put your mind to.

It is a verse in the Proverbs written by King Solomon. According to 1 Kings 3:11-14, God gave Solomon *"wisdom and understanding"* beyond what anyone "has had or ever will have!"

If you apply this verse to your plans and dreams, you will succeed and·achieve your goals.

Before we look at the verse, I want to give you a glimpse into King Solomon and what led to him becoming the wisest man who ever lived.

Solomon's Dad was King David. This is the same David who defeated the giant Goliath and was known as a man after God's own heart. Basically, when Solomon took over as King, he had huge shoes to fill.

We are told in scripture that *"The Lord appeared to Solomon during the night in a dream, and God said, 'Ask for whatever you want me to give you.'"*
—1 Kings 3:5

Solomon could have asked for anything. What would you have asked for?

*"**Give me an understanding heart so that I can govern your people well and know the difference between right and wrong.** The Lord was pleased that Solomon had asked for wisdom."* —1 Kings 3:9-10

Wow. He could have asked for wealth. He could have asked for fame. But Solomon asked for **wisdom** to help him do the right thing at the right time so that he could make a positive difference. This pleased God.

The Lord said, *"Because you have asked for wisdom in governing my people with justice and have not asked for a long life or wealth or the death of your enemies— **I will give you what you asked for! I will give you a wise and understanding heart such as no one else has had or ever will have! And I will also give you what you did not ask for**—riches and fame! No other king in all the world will be compared to you for the rest of your life! And if you follow me and obey my decrees and my commands as your father, David, did, I will give you a long life."* —1 Kings 3:11-14

Because King Solomon asked for wisdom, God granted him wisdom and understanding beyond what anyone else would ever have, and God also blessed him with so much more.

Now, briefly, look at the fruit that came out of Solomon's wisdom. We are told that while Solomon was King,*"The **people of Judah and Israel were as numerous** as the sand on the seashore. They were* *very contented, with* **plenty to eat and drink**." *—1 Kings 4:20*

Everyone in his nation had plenty to eat and drink. There was no lack.

The scripture says, *"During the lifetime of Solomon, all of Judah and Israel* **lived in peace and safety**. *And from Dan in the north to Beersheba in the south,* **each family had its own home and garden**." *—1 Kings 4:25*

Solomon's wisdom ensured there was no inequality. Everyone had a home and land. The nation also lived in peace and safety.

I pray that God will grant you big dreams and incredible insight to help you achieve your God-given dreams and become successful. But more than this, I pray that God will also positively impacts the lives of those who come across your path as you accomplish your dreams.

I am so grateful that God got the wisest man who has ever lived to write his wisdom down so that we can follow his principles. I want to focus on one scripture that, if applied, has the potential to set you on the path to success when it comes to achieving your dreams and goals.

These words of King Solomon come out of Proverbs 21:5...

"The plans of the diligent lead to profit as surely as haste leads to poverty." *—Proverbs 21:5 NIV*

According to Solomon, the "plans of the diligent led to profit."

To be **DILIGENT** means to...

- Plan carefully
- Focus on the task at hand and give it your full attention
- Work persistently
- Be industrious and conscientious
- Work towards being a person of excellence.

Diligence is not only planning well but working at your plan to ensure you accomplish your goal. It requires a bit of work. It is a skill you can learn.

According to Solomon, the flip side is that if you are not diligent and hurry to get to the result without a plan and strategy, it will inevitably fail and "leads to poverty."

A diligent person will plan well. This includes having good time management and scheduling important tasks that need to be done to achieve their dreams, goals, and objectives.

You cannot just daydream or fantasize your way to success. Yes, you need a dream, but a dream without a plan will not materialize. A lazy person often takes shortcuts and is too impatient to plan well, which leads to failure.

YOU NEED A STRATEGIC PLAN

A plan is your roadmap. If you have a plan and the determination to follow through, you can accomplish your goals.

God never works without a plan.

God gave Moses the plan for the Tabernacle. He gave Gideon a plan to win the battle. He gave Noah a plan to build an ark. God gave Joshua a plan to conquer Jericho, and He gave Solomon a plan to build the temple.

In the same way, you need a strategy to accomplish your goals.

In a nutshell, if you...

- Are diligent
- Plan carefully
- Work meticulously, not necessarily just hard, but work smartly
- Are disciplined
- Follow through
  ...you will more than likely prosper.

But if you...

- Don't have a plan
- Hurry and take easy shortcuts
- Are lazy and make poor decisions
- Don't follow through on your processes
  ...you will more than likely fail.

Let's examine the same scripture from the New Living Translation to get another perspective of what Solomon was saying here.

*"**Good planning and hard work lead to prosperity, but hasty shortcuts lead to poverty.**" —Proverbs 21:5*

No matter your goals, if you want to succeed, all you need to do is...

- Have a vision
- Set up a plan
- Strategize - create a process you can stick to
- Work at your plan
- Review your plan now and then - make sure you are still on track and make minor tweaks if you are not
- Follow through
  ...and you will succeed.

You will face roadblocks, but being diligent means keeping focused, staying motivated, and pushing through the obstacles until you achieve your desired outcome.

If you want to be successful, then follow King Solomon's advice. Let's break his advice down...

Bullet Points
What is your objective?
What are your dreams?
What are your goals?
Dream. Have a vision—set goals. Be specific.

How can you achieve your goals and dreams?
Where are you now?
Where do you want to end up?
Set up a plan to get you from where you are, to where you want to be.

In a nutshell, you need to be honest with where you are, and you need a clear picture of what you want to achieve. You need to be specific.

This will require looking at all the facts, assessing your options, getting the right advice, and setting up a realistic plan.

HOW CAN YOU ENSURE THAT YOU FOLLOW THROUGH?

- You need to set up a STRATEGY to help you stick to your goals and objectives.
- You need to BREAK IT DOWN into stepping-stones. One step at a time, done regularly over time, will help you develop the habit of following through.
- You need to MAKE IT EASY. Can you automate it? Can you make it part of your routine? Can you put it in your schedule?
- You need to REVIEW. If you can measure it, you can manage it. What is working? What can you change? Small tweaks from time to time will help you stay on track and help you to adapt your plan to achieve your goals and dreams.

"The plans of the diligent lead to profit as surely as haste leads to poverty." —Proverbs 21:5 NIV

"Good planning and hard work lead to prosperity, but hasty shortcuts lead to poverty." —Proverbs 21:5 NLT

Don't take shortcuts. Plan well. Work at your plan. Work smart. Put the right processes and systems in place. Follow through. And you will set yourself up to prosper.

In the next section of this book, I am going to help you develop a STEP-BY-STEP PLAN AND PROCESS to help you get from where you are to where you want to be.

DARE TO DREAM

66

***Write down the vision clearly on tablets,
so that even a runner can read it.***

Habakkuk 2:2

Chapter 10

THE POWER OF SETTING GOALS

Write Down Your Goals and Dreams.

Without having a dream or setting goals, you will drift aimlessly through life.

Failing to plan is planning to fail!

"Hope deferred makes the heart sick, but when dreams come true there is life and joy" —Proverbs 13:12

So, I want to encourage you to...

• Dare to dream
• Review your priorities
• Set goals so that you can build towards a brighter future

You cannot do much about your past. Whether it was good or bad, it is over. What has happened is gone. You can, however, do something about your future!

SOMETHING POWERFUL HAPPENS WHEN YOU WRITE DOWN YOUR GOALS

Write your goals down:

"And the Lord answered me and said, 'Write down

the vision clearly on tablets, so that even a runner can read it.'" —Habakkuk 2:2

When you write down your goals, not only does it help you commit to your goals, but it also helps you clarify what you want, and it will spur you on to take action.

THE POWER OF SETTING GOALS

I heard about research at a large university about 50 years ago. I do not know which university it was done at or who the Professor involved was, but the story inspired me to write down my future dreams and set goals.

According to the story, one day near the end of the term, the class professor sent half the students home an hour early. The balance of the class was instructed to write down their goals and aspirations for the future. After these students had finished the exercise, the Professor collected their papers and dismissed the class. Without reading his student's responses, he filed their notes, and nothing further was said of the exercise. This class graduated and continued their lives, many starting careers in various fields and having families.

After 20 years had passed, the Professor started his research. He checked in on each of his students who had graduated 20 years earlier and analyzed what they had achieved in their lives since graduation. He then reviewed the results, comparing those who had written down their goals against those who had not participated in the goal-writing exercise.

The results were startling...

According to the story, roughly 80% of those who took the time to write down their goals and aspirations succeeded and achieved them, while only around 20% of those who did not write down their goals ended up being successful.

A PERSONAL TESTIMONY

In early 2000, when Janet and I were newlyweds inspired by this story, we decided to write down our goals and aspirations. Just before we got married, I had recently settled my outstanding debt, which I shared earlier in the book. I had very little savings. At the time, we were living in a small two-bedroom apartment. We had one car between us and had to budget our money carefully to ensure we could put food on the table and cover our bills.

One night, we decided to write down our goals. We were very specific. We wrote down our financial and personal goals. These goals included that we wanted two cars. I wanted to drive a silver BMW. We dared to dream some big dreams. We wanted to own our own home in the suburbs with a double garage and a pool. We wanted enough money in savings for short-term emergencies and to have enough money invested each month to build toward financial freedom. We also wanted to have more than enough so that we could be a blessing to others, too. In our goal setting, we included how we wanted to be able to travel overseas. We also wrote down how we would love to have three children and be able to raise them well without any financial burdens. I also set ministry goals of wanting to reach those who were lost and hurting, bringing hope to others who were less fortunate than we were.

After writing down our goals and aspirations on a single piece of paper, we committed our goals to God. This paper was filed and forgotten about.

Two years later, we had our first child and moved into our new home in the suburbs. Another few years passed, and we now had three little boys running around. One day, out of the blue, about ten years later, I was searching for a book on our small bookshelf. As I pulled a book out, a discolored piece of paper wedged between two books fell out of the bookshelf.

It was the goals we had set when we first got married. As I read through the goals, I got goosebumps and I started to tear up. I sat there is absolute awe and gratitude. Guess what? Every single goal had come to pass.

We had three sons. We had our home in the suburbs. It had a double garage, and we had recently put in a pool. We had been on four international trips: one to Namibia, one to Mauritius, a cruise from Venice in Italy, and a trip to Spain. We had also managed to build up savings and investments.

On the ministry front, God had also opened doors and increased my influence, opening doors to minister and bring hope, with tens of thousands coming to

Christ and finding new life.

Since writing down our goals in 2000, we have continued to dare to dream and attempt greater things with God, and I have seen many more dreams and goals come to pass, including being blessed with a fourth son. I pray that many more of our dreams and aspirations will come true in the years to come.

I need to encourage you to write down your goals!

Take some time out to dream.

You may need to arrange a date night with your spouse. All you need to take with you is a pen and a piece of blank paper. Dare to dream. Chat through your hopes and aspirations that you want to achieve in the future.

Where do you see yourself in 5 years from now? In 10 years? 20 years?

In the following chapters, we will share a step-by-step process you can follow to ensure you bring your goals to fruition.

But for now...

All you need is to take time out to dream and set goals.

Dare to dream. Write down your goals. Be specific. Aim high.

Something powerful happens when you write down your goals!

66

May He give you the desires of your heart and make all your plans succeed.

Psalms 20:4

Chapter 11

YOUR GOAL SETTING PLAN

A Step-by-Step Plan to Turn Your Dreams
into Reality

It is important to set goals. Without setting goals, you will drift aimlessly and never achieve your hopes and dreams.

I know many who have set out to achieve their goals and dreams but have stopped short. People let go of their dreams for several reasons. Sometimes it is an obstacle. Sometimes, it is a lack of planning. Sometimes, life happens.

"Hope deferred makes the heart sick, but when dreams come true there is life and joy." —Proverbs 13:12

When dreams don't come to pass, they can leave you broken, frustrated, and hopeless. But when dreams come to fruition, there is life and joy. In this chapter, I want to share a simple step-by-step GOAL-SETTING strategy with you. It will help you stay on course. I have personally used this process many times, and I can assure you it works. If applied, this simple step-by-step goal-setting strategy will help you stay on course.

Today is the day of new beginnings. Today is the day you Lift the Lid. Today is the day you can set goals, dare to dream, and put plans in place to build towards a brighter future.

You cannot do much about your past. What has happened is gone! You can, however, do something about your future...

You don't have to be average or ordinary. When you dare to dream and start setting goals, you set yourself up for an extraordinary future.

IT IS NOW TIME TO GET STARTED!

Here are some Practical Steps to help you achieve your God-ordained Dreams.

STEP 1:
WHAT?

I would like to suggest a few ideas to help you set your goals:

WRITE DOWN YOUR GOALS

As mentioned in a previous chapter, I want to encourage you to write down your goals.

"And the Lord answered me and said, 'Write down the vision clearly on tablets, so that even a runner can read it.'" —Habakkuk 2:2

Not only will writing down your goals help to keep you committed, but something powerful happens when you take the time to put pen to paper and record your dreams and goals.

Answer the following question:

STEP 1: WHAT?

- What are your goals and dreams?
- What do you want?

"Where there is no vision, the people perish." — *Proverbs 29:18*

It is important to set goals for all the areas of your life. You need to see how all your dreams and goals fit together.

Below is a basic list of areas to consider...
(This list is to serve as a guide. Feel free to add any other goals you have.)

God goals:

- Time with God
- Reading God's Word and time in prayer
- Ministry goals

Health:

- Diet
- Fitness

Personal:

- Education
- Time for self

Family:

- Time with family
- Holiday
- A new home
- A new car
- Children's education

Financial:

- Eliminating debt
- Building up savings for short-term needs
- Building up a Wealth Portfolio for the future
- Retirement
- Own business

By including all your goals, it will force you to clarify what you want and motivate you to take action.

Take time to articulate your dreams and goals.

Brainstorm. Discuss your dreams with your loved ones.

Once you know what you want to achieve, you can put a PLAN in place to achieve it, but first, you need to answer the WHY.

WHY do you want it?

STEP 2:
WHY?

Once you know what you want to achieve, you need to answer the WHY.

Why do you want to achieve it? What is the reason?

Your WHY will help you define the purpose and gauge how important your dream or goal is to you.

Answer the following question:

STEP 2: WHY?

WHY do you want it?

Your WHY will help you get clarity on what you want.

Your WHY will help you articulate why this goal is important to you.

Your WHY will help you to get your priorities in the correct order.

Why do you want to achieve this? Why is this important? If it is a real dream, you will do something about it. If not, you never will.

Once you are sure of WHAT you want to achieve and WHY you want it, you need to determine by WHEN you want to achieve the goal. Only then can you put a PLAN in place to do this...

STEP 3:
WHEN?

Once you know WHAT you want to achieve and WHY you need to achieve it, you need to answer the WHEN.

WHEN would you want to achieve each of your goals and dreams?

Your WHEN will help you to set timelines.

Make sure that your timeline is realistic.

You may need to get advice to reach a particular goal. This will take place during the planning stage.

Remember, you can always go back and adjust your plan to ensure that your goals remain attainable and fit in with your lifestyle and budget constraints.

Answer the following question:

STEP 3: WHEN?

By WHEN do you want to reach your specific goal?

Your WHEN will help you set time frames.

Once you are sure of WHAT you want to achieve, WHY you want it, and have determined by WHEN you want to achieve the goal, you need to answer the HOW.

This is where you can put a PLAN in place to do this...

CLINTON J WERNER

STEP 4:
HOW?

How are you going to get there?

You need a **PLAN** - the **MAP** of how you can get from where you are to where you want to be.

Answer the following question:

STEP 4: HOW?

How can you achieve this goal within the set timeframe?

Your HOW is your PLAN.

Without a PLAN, your dreams will only be wishful thinking, leaving you frustrated.

Without a clear PLAN, you will probably battle to achieve your goals and dreams.

"Good planning and hard work lead to prosperity, but hasty shortcuts lead to poverty." —Proverbs 21:5

How will you achieve your dreams?

How will you realize your goals?

IF YOU WANT TO TURN YOUR DREAMS INTO REALITY, SIMPLY ASK YOURSELF...

- WHAT are my dreams and goals?
- WHY do I want to achieve them?
- By WHEN do I plan to achieve them?
- HOW can I make these dreams and goals a reality?

- First decide on WHAT you want to achieve.
- Then make sure you know WHY you want it.
- Then you need to determine by WHEN you want to achieve the specific goals.
- You can then answer the HOW and formulate a plan so that you can start working towards making your dreams a reality.

IF YOU FOLLOW THESE 4 SIMPLE STEPS, YOU WILL SET UP A PLAN TO ACHIEVE YOUR GOALS

If you apply this step-by-step approach, you will set yourself on the journey to achieve your dreams and make them a reality.

Don't be lazy...
"Lazy people are soon poor;
hard workers get rich." —Proverbs 10:4

Work hard and prosper...
"Lazy people want much but get little, but those who work hard will prosper." —Proverbs 13:4

Set your goals. Dare to dream! Aim high. Attempt great things! May God bless you as you press forward, onwards and upwards, to make your dreams and goals a reality.

Before we move forward, there is another step that many don't take, which I suggest you apply to your goals and dreams. Many have good plans but find it difficult to follow through. This ONE step can literally be the difference between achieving your goals and giving up on your dreams.

Unfortunately, many still stumble along, and even with a plan, they battle to bring it to pass...

If you seriously want to accomplish your goals and dreams, you need to make a FIRM DECISION to DO or NOT DO something. You need to be DETERMINED to follow through.

Once you have your GOAL-SETTING PLAN in place and have made the FIRM DECISION to follow through, there is a vital step that you need to apply to make it easier for you to stick to your plan and follow through. It is all about THE SYSTEM.

In the next chapter, we will look at this vital strategy that will help make it easy for you to achieve your goals.

We will then share the final **missing ingredient** that many are not aware of, that can make the biggest difference of all, which has the potential to supernaturally catapult you into your God-ordained destiny.

66

Finishing is better than starting.
Patience is better than pride.

Ecclesiastes 7:8

Chapter 12

THE SYSTEM

The Vital Cog That Turns Your Plans
into an Easy-to-Follow Process

By now, I hope that your dreams and goals for the future are starting to take shape.

I also hope you have asked the right questions to help SET YOUR GOALS so you can DEVELOP A STRATEGIC PLAN...

- WHAT are my goals and dreams?
- WHY do I want to achieve them?
- By WHEN do you plan to achieve them?
- HOW can I make these dreams and goals a reality?

These questions will help you to prioritize your goals and construct a plan of action to help you achieve your dreams and goals.

Your strategic plan is your long-term step-by-step blueprint of what you need to do to accomplish your goals and make your dreams a reality.

"Good planning and hard work lead to prosperity, but hasty shortcuts lead to poverty." —Proverbs 21:5

With a dream and a plan, you are 80% there. But the vital, often missing, cog in the wheel is all about developing a SYSTEM to help you stick to your process.

A SYSTEM is simply a set of links that work together as parts of a mechanism. Your system is about building good habits and implementing a simple step-by-step process to turn your dreams and goals into reality.

We have already touched on the importance of FORMING GOOD HABITS. I want to elaborate on this:

It can be tough work trying to implement a new set of habits. Many give up following their plans to make their dreams a reality because it seems too much effort and work. It can seem overwhelming to make changes and stick to new plans. It can seem complicated to build new habits into your routine. Unless you MAKE IT EASY you will battle to follow through on your plans.

This is why it is vital that you create a system that will spur you on to stick to your plans and help you achieve your goals.

Once you build your system it will become part of your routine, and simply a way of life.

Good habits usually lead to success, while bad habits lead to destruction.

"There is a time for everything, and a season for every activity under the heavens: A time to be born and a time to die, a time to plant and a time to uproot, a time to tear down and a time to build." —Ecclesiastes 3:1-3

It is time to tear down your destructive habits and build some good ones.

Your habits, whether good or bad, will impact your future, either for the better or the worse. I encourage you to form GOOD HABITS, which can help you make good decisions to succeed.

The decisions you make today will determine your tomorrow. Many of the choices we make will lead to a predictable outcome.

If you keep following your current path, where will you end up?

Join the dots!

What road are you on?

"A wise person chooses the right road. A fool takes the wrong one." —Ecclesiastes 10:2

The good news is that you can change. No matter who you are, where you find yourself, or what you have done or not done, you can build good habits.

In other words, you can change if you do not like how your life is going. You are one decision away from your best decision ever. And you do not need to do it alone – God wants to walk the journey with you.

You cannot change your past, but you can change your habits and rewrite your story.

It is often challenging to start when you change your habits, but if you practice good habits, regularly repeat them, and let them become part of your daily routine, you'll adjust. Eventually, they will become part of your usual way of life.

When you make consistent choices, you form a foundation for your habits.

Successful people have successful habits, while unsuccessful people have unsuccessful habits.

A habit is something...

- You practice,
- Keep repeating,
- Which becomes an easy routine,
- And eventually a way of life!

CUT A NEW PATH

What do you want to achieve in life?
What are your goals?

- Do you want to reach your world?
- Do you want to get out of debt?
- Do you want to save?
- Do you want financial freedom?
- Do you want to get into shape?
- Do you want to build your business?
- Do you want to develop a better relationship with God or your loved ones?

If so, set the goal, develop a plan, and set up the structure that you need to change your habits.

If you want something you have never had, you have to do something you have never done!

Practice your new habits. It may be challenging, but I need to encourage you to keep on pressing on! Eventually, your new good habit will become a routine and a way of life.

FOLLOW THROUGH

I know it is easy to start something, but you need to follow through. Be committed to your new habits and stick to your plan.

It would be best if you had a **no-exception policy** so that you stick to your new habits no matter what happens.

Get disciplined. Get determined.

Sometimes, it is good to be flexible, but when it comes to your goals and dreams, you must be **inflexible**. Don't compromise. Be single-minded. Make your habit a consistent practice until it becomes part of your way of life.

GOOD INTENTIONS ARE NOT ENOUGH

At the start of a New Year, many make New Year Resolutions. Many quickly set their goals for the New Year but are not so good at following through...

By the way, do you know what a resolution is?

A RESOLUTION is making a FIRM DECISION to DO or NOT DO something. It is to be persistent or DETERMINED.

Your dreams and goals for the future cannot just be a casual wish. It would be best to make a firm, determined decision to follow through.

At the start of last year, a friend of mine, Bob, posted that starting 1 January, he would run 5 km daily. A month into the new year, he had not even started running yet!

In the same way, I know many who have dreams they so dearly want to achieve but have not followed through.

Here is the crux: You need to develop an AUTOMATED SYSTEM consisting of good habits that are EASY to accomplish and can help you FOLLOW THROUGH to reach your dreams.

Some see setting goals as a waste of time because they never follow through. Many start with good intentions but often struggle to follow through.

In his bestselling book, Atomic Habits, which I recommend you read to form good habits, James Clear said, *"Goals are good for setting a direction, but systems are best for making progress." He said, "Don't just focus on your goals, but focus on your system instead."*

If you want to succeed at seeing your dreams and goals pass, you need to...

- DARE TO DREAM
- SET UP A PLAN TO ACHIEVE YOUR GOALS
- BUILD GOOD HABITS
- BE RESOLUTE – MAKE A DETERMINED DECISION TO FOLLOW THROUGH
- DEVELOP YOUR SYSTEM

YOUR SYSTEM

To set up a system that will work for you, you need to look at your dreams, plan, and create a simple **STEP-BY-STEP PROCESS** that you can build into your life.

Your process needs to be **EASY-TO-FOLLOW** and must become a habit, a part of your **REGULAR ROUTINE**, so that it becomes **AUTOMATIC.**

It is good to set goals and have big dreams. This is an important starting point, but all the good intentions will not bring your plans to fruition without YOUR SYSTEM.

If you can get your system working, you will make it easy to get from where you are to where you want to be with the least effort possible.

MAKE IT EASY TO ACHIEVE YOUR GOALS

I want you to consider 7 questions that can make it easier to develop a winning strategy...

1. What ADVICE do you need?

Getting advice from the right person can make it easy to achieve your goals and make your life much easier.

If you want to lose weight, you should seek guidance from your doctor. It is often prudent to meet with a dietician who can help construct an eating plan. Sitting with a personal trainer and developing an exercise program would also be a good idea.

If your goal is to build wealth or save up for a specific dream, then meet with a Financial Advisor who can comprehensively analyze where you are and what you need to do to achieve your goal.

Whether it be building up enough money to fund an international family holiday five years from now, wanting to buy your dream home, or planning to save up sufficient wealth for your retirement, a Financial Advisor will be able to help you construct a realistic and achievable plan to help you make your dream come to reality, while also ensuring that you have the proper protections in place on the road towards financial freedom.

A Financial Advisor can also help you come up with the most appropriate structure and fund selection to help you achieve your specific goals.

If you want to settle your debt, you must chat with your banker. Get a complete overview of what you owe and some advice on how you can pay off your debt within a certain period.

Seeking a professional's ADVICE will make it easier to accomplish your plans.

2. What do you need to ELIMINATE?

To make it easy to achieve your goals, you may need to eliminate some things that are getting in the way and sabotaging your plans.

If your goal is to lose a load of weight, but your cupboards are full of junk food, you will have a continual battle.

If you want to settle debt or build up a wealth portfolio, you must review your budget. What non-essentials can you cut out of your budget for a season to **free up space** so you can use the extra cash to squash your debt or build up your savings and investments?

If you can ELIMINATE the temptations, the time wasters, and dream-destroyers, you will have a much better chance of following through.

What are the dream-stealers that you need to eliminate?

3. What do you need to ADD?

To make it easy to achieve your goals, you may need to get a few items to make it easier to stick to your plans.

If you want to start training, you may need to invest in running shoes.

If you want to lose weight, you may need to buy a scale.

If you plan to eat better, you should stock your cupboards with healthy foods.

What do you need to ADD?

4. What can you AUTOMATE?

Imagine if you could set up a system that will automatically lead to achieving your goals...

This is possible with many of your financial goals. Once you know how much and where you will invest to achieve a specific purpose, you can automate it by setting up a bank debit or stop order. This will ensure that the money allocated to your goal is automatically deducted from your bank account each month on a specific date before you are tempted to spend that money.

You will then make it easy to achieve your financial dreams without the hassle of automating.

5. Can you SCHEDULE it?

If you want to follow through on your plans, it would be best to put it in your diary, making it easy to achieve your goals.

Book the time out if you exercise four times a week. If you don't schedule it, something else will come up and prevent you from following through.

If you want to rekindle the flame in your marriage, you may need to schedule a weekly date night. If you don't plan it, it just won't happen.

If you plan to work on your walk with God, maybe you need to get up an hour before the rest of the family and spend some time praying and reading your Bible. If you don't set the alarm earlier or schedule it, you will battle to follow through.

What do you need to SCHEDULE in your diary?

6. Can you add ACCOUNTABILITY?

If you are accountable to the right people, there is a higher chance that you will achieve your goal.

If your goal is to lose weight, can you schedule a weekly weigh-in to keep yourself accountable?

If you plan to go to the gym at 6 am, can you get a friend to join you? You won't be tempted to sleep in if you have to meet your friend at the gym.

What can you do to build ACCOUNTABILITY into your plans?

7. Can you PREPARE well?

If you prepare well, you can make it easy to follow through.

If you plan to run each morning, it would help if you set out your running shoes the night before.

To build wealth, you must keep a close eye on your finances.

If you plan to reduce your social media time, turn your phone off and leave it in the kitchen.

If you plan to lose weight, stock your fridge and cupboards with health foods.

If you plan to spend time with God each night before bed, put your Bible beside your bed.

By PREPARING well, you will make it easier to follow through on your goals.

CONSIDER HABIT STACKING

We live in an unbelievably busy world, with continual commitments demanding our time and attention. Time is limited. I know you have a life to live, and fitting all your plans in can be seriously challenging. In order to achieve your dreams, consider **habit-stacking**. This involves combining certain activities to free up time and "kill two birds with one stone", as the saying goes.

Can you combine a few related tasks?

If you want to build on your **prayer** life, take time out to **relax** while doing some **exercise**, and need to take your dog for a walk, can you combine this into a daily prayer walk?

You will be taking time out to breathe, exercise, and walk your dog, while spending time with God in prayer, all at the same time.

If you want to start spending more time as a family and you are looking to grow spiritually, could you consider going to Church or a cell group as a family?

If you plan to read a book a month and want to exercise, can you do an hour cycle on a stationary bike and do your reading simultaneously?

HABIT STACKING can allow you to combine similar tasks, freeing time and making it easy to follow through.

ADD TRIGGERS

Can you create TRIGGERS?

Triggers can help you to stick to your plans.

When you wake up, you probably do some things automatically. Maybe you make coffee or take a shower. Many follow the same routine each day without even realizing it.

Can you use certain moments in the day as triggers to get started on your goals?

Every morning, after making your coffee, can you use this as a trigger to spend time with God?

If you take lunch at 1 pm, can you use this as a trigger to spend 2 minutes praying for your family or a specific need?

Your TRIGGER can be anything to remind you to follow through on your goal. When you build the triggers into your schedule, they will eventually become part of your daily routine.

THE GOYA PRINCIPLE

Many years ago, at a company conference, a marketing guru shared how procrastination is one of the biggest killers of people following through on achieving their plans.

The presenter shared his antidote to procrastination. It was called the GOYA principle.

It was simply that you need to "Get Off Your Ass."

While this acronym may be a little tactless or disrespectful, it does drive the point home that to achieve your goals, you need to get up and get moving.

Like a rocket about to take off, you must prepare to fly.

5-4-3-2-1

Blast off!

BACK TO BOB

At the start of this chapter, I told you about my friend, Bob, who set the goal of running 5 km every day, but a month after setting the plan, he had not even put his running shoes on yet.

If Bob had developed a system, he would have had a greater chance of achieving his goal.

Let me show you how...

1. Bob has a GOAL of running 5 km per day. ✔

2. Bob needs to make a FIRM DECISION to follow through. ✔
3. Bob needs a PLAN. He must decide on a route he will run and get a pair of running shoes. ✔
4. Bob now needs a SYSTEM...

Let's help Bob create an easy-to-follow system to help him achieve his goal...

- Bob needs to **prepare well** by setting out his running shoes before he goes to bed.
- Bob can create a **trigger** by setting his alarm each morning an hour earlier to make time to run.
- Bob needs to **schedule the time** to run each morning in his diary.
- Bob can make it **more realistic** by choosing to run four times a week.
- Bob could ask a friend to join him. By running with a friend, he will be kept **accountable** and make it fun. Alternatively, Bob could **habit stack** by listening to an audiobook while doing his run.

If Bob included a few of the steps above, he would make it much easier to follow through on his plan. ✔

I am confident that if Bob sticks to this process and makes it a part of his routine, it will become a life-changing habit to help him achieve his goal. ✔

My friend would stick to his 5 km per day running goal if he followed this process and made it a part of his daily routine. Over time, it would become second nature, a habit like brushing his teeth. He can then turn his New Year's Resolution into Reality.

In a nutshell, if you want to achieve your goals, you need to create YOUR SYSTEM.

Your system is a simple, easy-to-follow, step-by-step process that you regularly repeat as part of your life.

We will shortly bring this all together and include YOUR ACTION PLAN of how you can take your DREAMS, SET YOUR GOALS, and create YOUR SYSTEM.

But before we get there, I need to share THE MISSING KEY that many do not consider, which is often neglected. This KEY has the potential to unlock your destiny, bring supernatural acceleration, and change everything.

66

***Commit your work to the Lord
and then your plans will succeed.***

Proverbs 16:3

Chapter 13

THE MISSING KEY

Commit Your Plans to God.

There is a commonly overlooked KEY that can unlock your destiny and open doors that can supernaturally accelerate you into achieving your God-ordained dreams and goals.

The KEY is to **COMMIT YOUR GOALS AND DREAMS TO GOD.**

God wants a day-by-day relationship with you. He can do the impossible. He does not want you to do it alone. He wants you to bother Him with your problems. He gives wisdom. He leads and guides. He is interested in you and wants to be part of all your decisions.

I want to share a few powerful scriptures that clearly reveal THE KEY...

"Trust in the Lord and do good. Then you will live safely in the land and prosper. Take delight in the Lord, and He will give you your heart's desires." — *Psalm 37:3-4*

God's word is clear. When you trust God and do good, you will live in peace and prosper, or put another way, you will be successful.

And, when you put God first and live to please Him, delighting in Him, He will give you your heart's desires.

God's word continues, "**Commit everything you do to the Lord. Trust Him, and He will help you**." —*Psalm 37:3-5*

You can trust God. Commit everything to Him: your dreams, goals, ambitions, and your life, and He will help you bring it to pass.

What a powerful promise.

If you dare to dream and construct a plan with a step-by-step system, you are well on your way to achieving your dreams.

But don't go at your plans alone. Invite God to be the central part of your dreams, ambitions, and plans. He wants to help you set a winning strategy. He wants to see you succeed. So, commit your plans to God, and He will help you.

THE PRAYER OF JABEZ

In 1 Chronicles 4, hidden between a list of names, we find a few verses about a man named Jabez.

The name Jabez means pain. I don't know what happened in his home when he was born, but his mother named him pain. With a name like that, you would not think he would amount to much in life.

But we are told that Jabez was an honorable man, and even though he had caused pain and was in pain, he cried out to God to bless him.

"Now Jabez was more honorable than his

brothers. His mother had named him Jabez, saying, 'Because I bore him in pain.' Jabez cried out to the God of Israel, **'Oh, that you would bless me and enlarge my territory! Let your hand be with me and keep me from harm so that I will be free from pain.' And God granted his request**.*" —1 Chronicles 4:9-10*

Jabez asked God...
- Lord, please bless me (in other words: Lord, please empower me to prosper)
- Enlarge my territory (in other words: Lord, please give me a bigger vision, grant me influence, and give me greater capacity)
- Let your hand be on me (in other words: Lord, please grant me favor and success)
- Keep me from harm and pain (in other words: Lord, please protect me, let me be free from pain, and let me not cause pain)

Jabez simply asked God to pour out His blessing on every area of his life.   Jabez asked God, "Lord, please bless me, so that I can be successful and be a blessing to others."

And the Bible says, *"**God answered Jabez and granted his request**."*

No matter where you find yourself today. No matter how painful your life may have been up until now. Even if you have caused pain, ask God to bless you. Ask God to increase your influence and enlarge your territory. Ask God to keep you from harm and pain. Ask God to put his hand of protection and favor on you.

Let me **tell you a story about a young man and his rich dad.**

There was a young man who came from the upper end of society. His father was a very wealthy business tycoon. He was a generous and kind man. He loved his family, and he was admired by many. This young man always wanted to live independently. He chose not to join his father's business empire but instead went off on his own way. Although his business started well, he took a few hard knocks and ended up in a financial crisis. A close friend told him to contact his father and ask for some advice and financial assistance, but being too proud, he never did. A few months passed, and with the chaos in the markets, things went from bad to worse. He eventually got to the stage where he was flat broke, and his business was about to enter bankruptcy. His friend pleaded with him, "Call your father. He will help you." But the young man declined the advice. His business eventually collapsed, and he was left destitute.

You may say, "What a silly young man. Why didn't he just put his pride in his pocket and contact his dad? Why didn't he call on his father for help? After all, his dad was a generous man and would have gone out of his way to help his son."

You may think this young man was stupid, but it is no different to you and me when we battle through life and don't ask our Father in Heaven for help. After all, our God is merciful and kind and He wants the best for His children.

DON'T DO IT ALONE

You don't have to face life alone. Ask God to help you.

He is abounding in love. He is happy for you to bother Him with your problems. In fact, he is interested in every detail of your life. He wants to do life with you.

God is Our Father

"The LORD is like a father to his children, tender and compassionate to those who fear Him." —*Psalm 103:13*

"If you need wisdom, ask our generous God, and He will give it to you. He will not rebuke you for asking." —*James 1:5*

You do not need to face life alone. Ask God to place his hand of favor on your life and to bless you abundantly.

Often, we don't ask God to help us. God's word is clear, *"You do not have because you do not ask God."* —*James 4:2*

Jesus told us, *"Ask and it will be given to you; seek and you will find; knock and the door will be opened to you. For everyone who asks receives; the one who seeks finds; and to the one who knocks, the door will be opened."* —*Matthew 7:7-8*

Jesus also told us, *"Ask, using my name, and you will receive, and you will have abundant joy."* —*John 16:24*

Don't go after your dreams in your own strength. Place your life in Jesus' hands. Ask God to bless you, to enlarge your territory, to place His hand on you, to keep you from harm and pain, and to help bring your dreams to pass.

May God grant you the desires of your heart as you delight in Him.

God is in control

Do you realize how big God is?

God created the universe. He spoke light into darkness. He flung the stars into space. He made the animals, insects, birds, and the bees. He made the mountains, hills, rivers, and the sea. And He made you. He knows what is happening in this world and what is happening in your life. He also knows what will happen in the future.

Nothing is too hard for God. He can do the impossible. He is the way maker.

The Bible tells us, *"Do not wear yourself out to get rich, do not trust in your own cleverness." —Proverbs 23:4*

Rather, trust God. Rest in God.

Follow God's leading.

"Many are the plans in a person's heart, but it is the Lord's purpose that prevails." —Psalm 19:21

Remember that unless God is in it, your plans are useless.

*"**Unless the Lord builds the house, the builders labor in vain**." —Psalm 127:1*

Know that with God at your side, you can achieve your goals.

"I can do all things through Christ who gives me strength." —Philippians 4:13

God can do all things.

God can make a *"roadway in the wilderness."* He can make *"rivers flow in the desert."* —Isaiah 43:19

We are also told, *"And you shall remember the Lord your God, for it is He who gives you power to get wealth."* —Deuteronomy 8:18

God has all power and authority. He is the inventor of life. He can do the impossible. His wisdom is beyond ours, and He invites us to commit our plans to Him. When we do, He offers to help us. **This is a game-changer.** This KEY has the potential to catapult you into your God-ordained destiny.

THE KEY IS SIMPLE

God wants to be the center of your life and plans. Don't try to go after your dreams and goals alone. God wants you to bother Him with your problems. He longs to walk the journey with you. God is interested in you and has a plan for your life. He is interested in every area of your life.

So, make certain that you invite God to be part of your process. Share your goals and dreams with Him. Allow God, who has all the "know-how" to lead and guide you. After all, He knows what is up and what is around the next corner, and He has your best interest at heart.

COMMIT YOUR PLANS TO GOD

Let me share one more scripture with you that sums this up.

"Commit your actions to the LORD and your plans will succeed." —*Proverbs 16:3*

God's word is clear. Do not try to do everything in your own strength. Trust God.

Commit your plans to Him. Trust in Him, follow His direction, and He will lead you on the best pathway for your life. God brings success. God will help bring your plans to pass.

So, dare to dream. Write down your goals—set plans. Develop a strategy. And above all else, don't forget to commit your dreams, goals, and plans to God.

Something powerful happens when you commit your plans to God!

DARE TO DREAM

66

Be sure you know
the condition of your flocks,
give careful attention to your herds.

Proverbs 27:23

Chapter 14

REVIEW

Review Your Progress at Regular Intervals.

It is important to review your goals and your plans from time to time.

I suggest you review your progress regularly, whether it be quarterly or annually. When you measure your progress, it will help you remain on track.

REFLECT

How are your plans panning out?

It is good to look back and assess how things are going.

At times, you may go through a purple patch where everything works out, and you end up ahead of the curve. At times like this, celebrate, and keep pushing.

Other times, you may run into obstacles that slow you down, setting you back in your plans. It is okay. That is life. At times like this, adjust. Realign. Make sure that you stay on course. Don't slack off. Keep pressing on, onwards, upwards, one step at a time.

If your plans are not working, go back to the drawing board. Rework your plan and system.

If you have messed up or made poor decisions, face the music. Don't give up! Don't bury your head in the sand and pretend your problems don't exist. Rather, face it. Be honest with yourself. You can get back on track.

No matter how bad things have been, you can turn it around. If your plans have not worked, use this time to honestly reflect on your dreams and goals and consider a new approach. Just like how we discussed in the Vector Principle, tiny changes can lead to huge outcomes over the long term.

REVIEW

You need to assess where you are at various intervals.

What do the numbers look like?

How have things gone over the last quarter, over the last year, five years, ten years?

Remember, *"If you can measure it, you can manage it."*

It is vital to keep good records.

KNOW THE CONDITION OF YOUR PORTFOLIO

"Be sure you know the condition of your flocks, give careful attention to your herds; for riches do not endure forever, and a crown is not secure for all generations." —Proverbs 27:23-27

King Solomon told us we need to know the value of our "flocks." This was in farming terms. Today, you need to know the value of your "stocks."

Most people overestimate their wealth and underestimate their debt levels.

Do you know how much debt you have? Do you know the value of your wealth portfolio?

It is essential to track your goals. You need to know what is happening.

If you manage your plans well and regularly monitor where you are on your journey towards achieving your goals, you can prevent loss and make the necessary adjustments to stay on track.

It's important to know the condition of your "flocks."

Ask yourself...

- What is my end goal?
- Where am I now?
- Am I winning or losing?
- Am I ahead of target or behind?
- What is working?
- What is not working?
- What needs to change?

Document the results every quarter and every year, look back, and compare the results.

When you review your progress, you will be pleasantly surprised at how well you are doing if you stick to your system over time. This will motivate you to keep going.

Remember, the accumulation of your small steps, compounded over time, will lead to you accomplishing your goals and making your dreams a reality.

Examine how things are going and make sure that you stay on course.

As my good friend Andy always says, "If you can measure it, you can manage it!"

DARE TO DREAM

66

***Take delight in the Lord,
and He will give you the
desires of your heart.***

Proverbs 37:4

Chapter 15
PUT YOUR PLANS INTO PRACTICE

How to Put Your Plans into Practice.

I t starts with a dream. You then need to set the goals. The vital cog is creating a system that will make it easy for you to follow through.

We all have different dreams and goals:

- *Your goal may be to lose a lot of weight and get fit.*
- *Your dream may be to become debt-free because you are sick and tired of living under financial stress.*
- *Your goal may be to build towards financial freedom.*
- *Your dream may be to own your own home or drive a certain car.*
- *Your goal may be saving to build up money to cover your emergency needs.*
- *Your dream may be to build up enough money to take your family on an international holiday.*
- *Your goal may be to grow closer to God.*
- *Your goal may be to build closer relationships with your family and friends.*

- *Your dream may be to go to the Olympics, win Wimbledon, or make the World Cup team.*
- *Your dream may be to be president.*
- *Your goal may be to win the world for Christ.*
- *Your goal may be to live a balanced life.*

Whatever your dreams and goals are, you need to develop a PLAN and a SYSTEM.

Here is a practical summary of the process that you can follow...

RECORD YOUR DREAMS

- Something powerful happens when you WRITE DOWN YOUR DREAMS.
- Be SPECIFIC.

YOUR GOAL-SETTING PLAN

- WHAT are my dreams and goals?
- WHY do I want to achieve them?
- By WHEN do I plan to achieve them?
- HOW can I make these dreams and goals a reality?

YOUR SYSTEM

- A STEP-BY-STEP PROCESS.
- STEPPING-STONES that are EASY TO FOLLOW.
- Build in TRIGGERS and consider HABIT STACKING.
- Can you AUTOMATE?

- Build GOOD HABITS that eventually become part of your REGULAR ROUTINE

THE MISSING KEY
- COMMIT your dreams and plans TO GOD.
- God wants you to REACH YOUR DESTINY.

REVIEW
- RECORD your results.
- MEASURE it. Know your NUMBERS.
- REVIEW your progress.
- What needs to CHANGE? What needs to be REALIGNED?

Your personal action plan follows...

PERSONAL GOAL-SETTING ACTION PLAN WORKSHEET *(FREE DOWNLOAD)*

Here is a goal-setting action plan I have put together to help you create a simple, step-by-step guide to achieving your God-given goals and dreams. If you want a copy, **visit the resources page** on betteryouliving.com

BETTER**YOU**LIVING

DARE TO DREAM

PERSONAL GOAL-SETTING
ACTION PLAN

*A simple step-by-step guide for achieving
your God-given goals and dreams.*

A **betteryouliving.com** resource

DARE TO DREAM
Aim high. Lift the lid.

- Without setting goals, you will drift aimlessly and never achieve your dreams.

- Setting goals is important because it will force you to clarify what you want, and it will motivate you to take action.

- Something powerful happens when you write down your goals...

PERSONAL GOAL-SETTING
ACTION PLAN
A **betteryouliving.com** resource

DREAMS AND GOALS:

Make a Firm Decision to Go After Your Dreams.

WHAT?

• What are your goals and dreams?

• What do you want?

Answer here:

"Where there is no vision, the people perish."
Proverbs 29:18

PERSONAL GOAL-SETTING
ACTION PLAN

A *betteryouliving.com* resource

REASON AND PURPOSE:

Clarify Why it is Important

WHY?

- Why do you want to achieve this goal?
- What is the reason?

Answer here:

*"I have the right to do anything," you say—
but not everything is beneficial.*
1 Corinthians 6:12

PERSONAL GOAL-SETTING
ACTION PLAN

A **betteryouliving.com** resource

TIMELINE:

How Long Am I Giving Myself to
Accomplish My Goal?

WHEN?

• When do I want to achieve this?

• Is the timeframe realistic?

Answer here:

*"There is a time for everything, and a season
for every activity under the heavens."*
Ecclesiastes 3:1

PERSONAL GOAL-SETTING
ACTION PLAN

A *betteryouliving.com* resource

MY STRATEGIC PLAN:

My Map to Reaching My Goals and Dreams.

HOW?

• How am I going to get there?

• Where am I now?

• What is needed to get there?

Answer here:

*"Good planning and hard work lead to prosperity,
but hasty shortcuts lead to poverty."*
Proverbs 21:5

PERSONAL GOAL-SETTING
MY SYSTEM

A *betteryouliving.com* resource

SET UP MY SYSTEM:

My Blueprint Step-by-Step Strategy.

STEPPING-STONES:

- Make wise choices.
- Form good habits that are part of my regular routine.
- Cut a new path.
- Make it easy.
- Automate. Build in triggers. Habit stack.

Write here:

*"Finishing is better than starting.
Patience is better than pride."*
Ecclesiastes 7:8

PERSONAL GOAL-SETTING
THE MISSING KEY
A *betteryouliving.com* resource

THE MISSING KEY:
Commit Your Dreams and Plans to God.

COMMIT IT TO GOD:
• Invite God to join you on your quest
  to achieving your goals.

Write here:

*"Commit your work to the Lord
and then your plans will succeed."*
Proverbs 16:3

PERSONAL GOAL-SETTING
ACTION PLAN

A *betteryouliving.com* resource

RECORD YOUR RESULTS:

If You can Measure it, You can Manage it.

HOW AM I DOING?

- Review your progress at regular intervals to stay on track.

- Where am I now? What progress have I made?

- What is working? What is not working? What needs to change?

- Document the results. What do the numbers look like?

- Realign. Stay on course.

Make notes here:

"Trust in The Lord and do good. Then you will live safely in the land and prosper. Take delight in The Lord and He will give you your heart's desires. Commit everything you do to the Lord. Trust Him, and He will help you."
Psalms 37:3-5

NOTES:

PART THREE

FINISHING STRONG!

66

Blessed is the one who perseveres under trial because, having stood the test, that person will receive the crown of life that the Lord has promised to those who love Him.

James 1:12

Chapter 16

DON'T LET GO OF YOUR DESTINY

Don't let the bumps of life knock you off course.

So many have a dream that has not been fulfilled. So many set out with good intentions, but life just happens, and they stop short of reaching their goals and dreams.

Maybe you once had great dreams for your future, but a few bumps in the road or hard knocks took you off course. Something may have broken down. Maybe it was a storm that took you off course. Maybe you just got distracted.

Whatever the cause, you need to dust yourself off, get back up, and get back on the road towards accomplishing your dreams. With God, you can turn your setback into a great comeback.

Don't stop halfway on the road to your destiny. You need to follow through with your dreams so that you can reach your God-given destiny.

In Genesis 11, it tells the story of Terah. He was Abram's father. *"One day, Terah took his son Abram, his daughter-in-law Sarai (his son Abram's wife), and his grandson Lot (his son Haran's child) and moved away from Ur of the Chaldeans. He was headed for the land of Canaan, but they stopped at Haran and settled there. Terah lived for 205 years and died while still in Haran."* —Genesis 11:31-32 NLT

Terah lived in Ur. He had a dream to move to Canaan - the promised land, a land of prosperity, flowing with milk and honey. Terah set out on a journey with his family to fulfill his destiny.

But do you know what the Bible says?

Terah stopped short. We are not sure what happened, but he settled in Haran. The Bible says that Terah lived for 205 years and died while still in Haran.

So many people set out to achieve their dreams, but due to problems or setbacks, they end up short.

While it is better to try and get halfway than not to try at all, we often stop short and end up not accomplishing our destiny, just like Terah. Instead of settling in the promised land, he stopped short and settled along the way.

I want to encourage you not to let go of your dreams. Don't let go of your destiny. Follow through.

If you have stopped short, go back to your dreams, go back to your destiny. Put a new plan in place, make a fresh commitment to God, and start moving forward.

GOD WANTS TO HELP YOU REACH YOUR DESTINY

Genesis 12 tells us that after Terah had died, God appeared to Abram (who later became Abraham) and told him it was time to move on.

"The Lord had said to Abram, 'Leave your native country, your relatives, and your father's family, and go to the land that I will show you.'" —Genesis 12:1

It seems like God wanted Abram to finish the journey his dad was supposed to accomplish. God wanted Abram to go to the promised land, the land flowing with milk and honey.

And God gave Abram an incredible promise. God told him, *"I will make you into a great nation. I will bless you and make you famous, and you will be a blessing to others, I will bless those who bless you and curse those who treat you with contempt. All the families on earth will be blessed through you."* — Genesis 12:2-3

God promised to bless Abram.

Abram obeyed God. He followed through.

"So, Abram departed as the Lord had instructed, and Lot went with him. Abram was seventy-five years old when he left Haran." —Genesis 12:4

Abram took over his father's destiny. It's as though God passed Terah's vision onto his son.

God promised to bless Abram and all people through him. This even includes you and me.

Now, along the journey, Abram faced droughts and famine. He faced danger and many crazy times, just like you and I will face on the road to our destiny.

But God was with Abram and blessed him abundantly.

Sometimes, Abram faced trials and probably

wanted to give up, but God encouraged him along the way and promised to be his protector.

God spoke to Abram. He comforted and guided him along the right path.

We are told, *"The Lord spoke to Abram in a vision and said to him, 'Do not be afraid, Abram, for I will protect you, and your reward will be great.'"—Genesis 15:1*

God will do the same for you. He wants a close walk with you.

DON'T FOCUS ON THE PROBLEMS, LOOK TO GOD

Now Abram didn't have a son. This was a big deal to him.

Abram asked God, *"O Sovereign Lord, what good are all your blessings when I don't even have a son?" —Genesis 15:2*

Basically, Abram was saying, "What's the point, Lord? If you bless me and I die, a servant in my household will inherit all my wealth."

God told Abram to look up...

"Then the Lord took Abram outside and said to him, 'Look up into the sky and count the stars if you can. That's how many descendants you will have!'" — Genesis 15:5-6

Today, God is telling you not to look at the problems around you but to look up to Him.

"And Abram believed the Lord, and the Lord counted him as righteous because of his faith." — Genesis 15:6

God gave Abram a vision. Not just that he would have a son but that God would give him many descendants.

"Then the Lord told him, 'I am the Lord who brought you out of Ur of the Chaldeans to give you this land as your possession.'" —Genesis 15:7

Don't let go of your destiny. Attempt great things with God and for God.

LOOK UP. COUNT THE STARS.

Just like God told Abram when revealing his purpose and plan for him, to "look up into the sky and count the stars," so God is calling you to dream again, to look up and see the possibility.

And, just like "Abram believed the Lord," you need to put your faith in God.

Don't allow your circumstances to cause limiting beliefs to cloud your vision. And don't limit God. He made you to be alive at this time. He is not finished with you. He made you with a purpose and will equip you to reach your destiny. Look up. Put your hope in God. Count the stars.

GOD HAS A GOOD PLAN FOR YOUR LIFE

Don't stop halfway. Dare to dream. Make certain that you continue to follow through. Make sure that you keep moving forward toward the destiny for which you were made.

Commit your life to God. Walk with Him. He will lead and guide you. He wants to direct you. He wants to help you, and He wants to encourage you along the journey.

The God who made the universe made you, and you are His prized possession.

He is interested in you. He wants you to be all that He made you to be. Do not live in dread. I know the world is uncertain, but don't abandon your purpose and dreams. Don't stop short. Follow through.

It is time for you to dream big dreams. You can begin again.

You can follow through with your dreams so that you can complete the purpose for which God made you.

DARE TO DREAM

66

*Brothers and sisters, I do not consider
myself yet to have taken hold of it.
But one thing I do: Forgetting what is behind
and straining toward what is ahead,
I press on toward the goal to win the prize
for which God has called me
heavenward in Christ Jesus.*

Philippians 3:13-14

Chapter 17

IT'S TIME TO BREAK CAMP

Let Go of What is Holding You Back.

I believe it is time for you to get ready so that you can move forward.

I am fully aware that many things will try to sabotage and hold you back from fulfilling your dreams, but I am convinced that God is able to catapult you forward, right into your God-given destiny.

One of my favorite Old Testament stories is found in the book of Exodus.

God's chosen people had let go of God and ended up in slavery and bondage. In their desperation, they cried out to God.

"But the Israelites continued to groan under their burden of slavery. They cried out for help, and their cry rose up to God. God heard their groaning, and He remembered his covenant promise to Abraham, Isaac, and Jacob. He looked down on the people of Israel and knew it was time to act." —Exodus 2:23-25

God heard their desperate cries, and He was moved.

Immediately, God set up a plan to save His people.

You can also cry out to God in the middle of your bondage. God wants you to bother Him with your problems - He wants to help you. He can set you free no matter where you find yourself. Nothing is too difficult for your Father in heaven. He is our deliverer. God can deliver you.

God orchestrated a plan to deliver his people. This included raising up Moses to lead them out of bondage, God also sent plagues on the land of Egypt to weaken its oppressive grip on his people. In the end, God set His people free.

At one time, darkness came over the whole land, yet God's children still *"had light in the places where they lived." —Exodus 10:23*

God can bring light into your darkest situation. He can make a way. He can help you accomplish your dreams no matter where you find yourself today or what you are going through.

God set up a miraculous plan to deliver His people. He even parted the Red Sea to make a way and lead His people out of bondage, on dry ground. God then destroyed the enemy by closing the sea on the chasing army.

Just like God opened the Red Sea, Jesus was lifted high on the cross, where He shed his blood so that you and I can be set free from bondage and be led into the promised land (heaven).

But let's backtrack a little. God spectacularly delivered His people from bondage. He then wiped out the enemy and brought His people to safety.

God planned to lead His people into a good land, the Promised Land, but He first led them into the wilderness. He wanted His people to get to know Him. God wanted to equip them for the Promised Land, which was their destiny.

God's plan was to get His people into the Promised Land without any major delays, but look at what happened!

"It takes eleven days to travel from Horeb by the way of Mount Seir to Kadesh-Barnea." —Deuteronomy 1:2

We are told that it usually would take only "eleven days" to travel from Mount Sinai into the Promised Land, but according to Joshua, *"The Israelites wandered in the wilderness for forty years." —Joshua 5:6*

An eleven day journey took God's people forty years to reach their Promised Land. You may ask why. We will get to this shortly.

Can you fathom this? Israel had cried out to God to deliver them. God had miraculously delivered His people.

It should have taken eleven days to get into the promised land, but forty years later, they were still camped in the wilderness. An entire generation missed out on the promised land!

Maybe you can resonate with God's people in the wilderness. You may have had a dream many years ago that you had every intention to reach, but maybe you are still in your wilderness. I don't know what happened to you. Was it the dream-stealer? Who interrupted or disrupted you from reaching your

Promised Land?

No matter what has happened, I believe God is going to help you get back on track. He can restore to you the years that have been stolen from you.

"I will restore to you the years that the swarming locust has eaten." —Joel 2:25

If your dream has been sabotaged and you still find yourself in the wilderness, don't give up on your destiny. Don't give in. It is time to lift the lid. Your best days are ahead of you.

By the way...

While in the desert, God continued to provide for and protect His people. He protected them with a pillar of fire by night and set up a cloud by day to shade them from the desert heat. He fed them with manna from heaven, and their clothes didn't even wear out!

In the same way, if you're still in your wilderness, God can provide!

DON'T GIVE UP ON YOUR DESTINY

After spending forty years in the wilderness, God told His people, *"It is time to break camp and move on." —Deuteronomy 1:7*

God told his people to move on to the Promised Land.

God continued, *"Look, I am giving all this land to you! Go in and occupy it, for it is the land the Lord swore to give to your ancestors Abraham, Isaac, and Jacob, and to all their descendants." —Deuteronomy 1:8*

IT IS TIME TO BREAK CAMP AND MOVE FORWARD

God told His people, "You have stayed here long enough. It is time to break camp and move forward."

I believe it is time for you to break camp and move on.

It is time to dream. It is time to leave your past behind. It is your time to get up and get ready to reach your dreams. No matter how bad things look, it is time to arise, break camp, and move forward.

PRESS ON

It is time to press ahead towards your God ordained goals.

"Brothers and sisters, I do not consider myself yet to have taken hold of it. But one thing I do: Forgetting what is behind and straining toward what is ahead, I press on toward the goal to win the prize for which God has called me heavenward in Christ Jesus." — *Philippians 3:13-14 NIV*

You don't have to face life alone. God wants to walk the journey with you right into your destiny.

WHAT IS HOLDING YOU BACK?

Israel had an eleven day journey from the wilderness to get into the promised land, but forty years later, they were still there.

Why?

God had given them the land, but what held them back?

What is holding you back and sabotaging your dreams?

Let us look at a few dream stealers that may be holding you back from fulfilling your God-given destiny. These include...

- Fear and unbelief
- Compromise
- Comfort
- Worry
- Unforgiveness, bitterness, and offense

We are going to unpack these areas that the enemy uses to sabotage your dreams so that you can be free.

Jesus said, *"And you will know the truth, and the truth will set you free." —John 8:32*

When these areas are dealt with, you can position yourself to move forward.

FEAR AND UNBELIEF

God had told His people that He was giving them the Promised Land.

While in the wilderness, Moses had sent twelve spies into the land to check things out. They came back with this report: *"We entered the land you sent us to explore, and it is indeed a bountiful country—a land flowing with milk and honey." —Numbers 13:27*

Although their destiny was bright and blessed, a land of abundance, God's people were held back by fear and unbelief.

Watch out for the BUT's in your life.

While the land was *"flowing with milk and honey,"* ten of the twelve spies spread a negative report that melted the people's hearts with fear.

They said, *"BUT the people living there are powerful, and their towns are large and fortified. We even saw giants there." —Numbers 13:28 NLT*

These ten negative spies continued, *"They are too strong."* In other words, "We are too weak!"

"We are like grasshoppers compared to them." They were saying, "They will wipe us out!" *—Numbers 13:31-33*

Two spies came back with a positive report. They came back saying, *"Let's go at once to take the land, we can certainly conquer it!" —Numbers 13:30*

These two spies, Caleb and Joshua, had faith in God. They believed that if God said they would have the land, it was theirs.

However, the fearful report of the other ten spies caused great fear among the people.

Fear will paralyze you and stop you from taking action.

The report of the ten pessimistic and unbelieving spies spread a fear which paralyzed God's people.

Don't bow down to fear, only bow down to God. If God says it, you can believe it and act on it. Always trust God.

How could God's people not trust Him?

God had mightily delivered them out of slavery. He had miraculously opened the Red Sea. He had led them out of bondage. He had promised His people this amazing Promised Land.

How could they not trust their God and Savior? After all, He has all power and authority in Heaven and on Earth.

Instead of trusting their limitless God, they let fear and unbelief hold them back.

A whole generation missed their destiny because of fear and unbelief.

No matter who you are or what you face, hold onto God. Don't fear. Put your faith in your strong and mighty God.

Fear paralyzes. It is the hypnotic power of the enemy. But God is bigger. He is stronger and mightier. God is greater than any crisis.

Don't let fear hold you back from your destiny. Are you being held back by fear? If so, put your hope in God.

"So do not fear, for I am with you; do not be dismayed, for I am your God. I will strengthen you and help you; I will uphold you with my righteous right hand." —Isaiah 41:10

"This is my command—be strong and courageous! Do not be afraid or discouraged. For the Lord your God is with you wherever you go." —Joshua 1:9

Don't let fear paralyze you. Follow Caleb and Joshua's example. Don't listen to the wrong voices. Listen to God. See your future with the eyes of faith. Be positive. Stand confidently on God's promises. Trust God.

It is time to...

- Shake off the fear
- Be brave
- Be strong
- Have courage
- Face your fear
- Walk through it
- Do it afraid
- Get moving
- Hold onto Jesus and push through

There is nothing to fear if God is with you. He is in complete control. Nothing can stand against God.

Most of your fears will never materialize. They are only negative images in your mind and illusions that the enemy uses to try to lead you off course. Don't let the enemy's deceptive tactics scare you, for his sole aim is to stop you from achieving your God-ordained dreams.

Remember, fear is only the imaginary deception from the enemy. Sometimes, you need to look fear dead in the face. Stand up. Act. Resist your fear. Just do it. Do it, afraid!

COMPROMISE

God's people became half-hearted and lukewarm. They compromised their relationship with God. They had more fear of man than faith in God.

Jesus warned us that in the last days, *"Sin will be rampant everywhere, and the love of many will grow cold." —Matthew 24:12*

If you have grown cold or become complacent in your walk with God, you can return to Jesus and begin again.

Jesus continued, *"But the one who endures to the end will be saved." —Matthew 24:13*

COMFORT

Although God had promised His people a land of blessing, they seemed to get too comfortable in the wilderness.

Don't let the comforts of life hold you back from your destiny.

It was an eleven day journey into the promised land from the wilderness, but forty years later, they were still camped in the desert.

What is holding you back from your God-given destiny? What is holding you back from your dreams?

Maybe it is something else like...

WORRY

The negative reports from the ten spies also made God's children worry. The uncertainty of what the future held made them anxious. This held God's people back from their "land flowing with milk and honey."

Worry is heavy. It will weigh you down and hinder you from following through on your goals and dreams.

"Worry will weigh you down." —Proverbs 12:25

Instead of worrying about everything and anything, you should rather pray about everything.

We are told, *"Don't worry about anything; instead, pray about everything. Tell God what you need, and thank Him for all He has done. Then you will experience God's peace, which exceeds anything we can understand. His peace will guard your hearts and minds as you live in Christ Jesus." —Philippians 4:6-7*

Surrender your worries to Jesus. He offers you a peace that surpasses all understanding.

You may also be anxious about the future. Are you troubled? Is worry holding you back from attaining your dreams and from living your life to the full? If so, give your worries to Jesus.

Jesus says, *"Come to me, all you who are weary and burdened, and I will give you rest." —Matthew 11:28*

UNFORGIVENESS, BITTERNESS AND OFFENSE

Also, watch out for bitterness, unforgiveness, and offense. Holding onto unforgiveness in your heart can cause so much trouble in your life. This will poison you and block you off from God's best. Bitterness, unforgiveness, and offense can poison your dreams and hold you back from reaching your destiny.

Look at what Jesus said about unforgiveness.

Jesus said, *"For if you forgive other people when they sin against you, your heavenly Father will also forgive you. But if you do not forgive others their sins, your Father will not forgive your sins."—Matthew 6:14-15*

According to Jesus, bitterness, offense, and unforgiveness can stop God from being able to forgive you.

God can move mountains in your life.

Jesus said, *"Have faith in God."* He went on and said, *"Truly I tell you, if anyone says to this mountain, 'Go, throw yourself into the sea,' and does not doubt in their heart but believes that what they say will happen, it will be done for them. Therefore, I tell you, whatever you ask for in prayer, believe that you have received it, and it will be yours."* —Matthew 11:22-24

God can do the impossible. He can launch you into your destiny. He can move mountains. He can make a way even when there seems to be no way, BUT this scripture continues with a stern warning.

"And when you stand praying, if you hold anything against anyone, forgive them, so that your Father in heaven may forgive you your sins." —Mark 11:25

In other words, holding onto bitterness and having unforgiveness in your heart can stop God from moving mountains and doing miracles in your life. It can even get in the way of you achieving your dreams.

Life is too short to get bitter and twisted. Forgive. Let go.

LET GO OF THE BLOCKAGES AND LET GOD IN

Maybe you are fearful and are filled with unbelief. Maybe you have compromised your walk with God. You may have become too comfortable. Perhaps you are gripped with worry. You may be held hostage by unforgiveness, bitterness, and offense, poisoning your life and dreams. Maybe your life is contaminated with other "stuff" causing great damage.

You need to let this go and surrender these things to God. You need to break camp and move forward.

If this sums up your life, why don't you surrender these things to God? These areas will not only ruin and sabotage your dreams but will also wreck your life and put your eternity at risk.

What is sabotaging your dreams and damaging your life? I need to implore you to surrender them to God.

LET GO. LET GOD.

Today, you can ask God to break off the strongholds of fear and limiting beliefs that are holding you back and put your hope in God.

You can let go of compromise and get fully connected to God. You can move forward out of your comfort zone and dare to dream once again. You can let go of worry and ask God to fill you with his peace and joy.

You can let go of bitterness and forgive, allowing God to move mountains in your way.

Today, you can let go of the areas in your life that are sabotaging your dreams and holding you back from your God-given destiny. You can ask God to set you free so that you can move forward...

Let us pray...

Dear Father God, you know me through and through. Point out anything negatively impacting my walk with you, and show me what is holding me back from achieving my God-given dreams and destiny.

Lord, today, I choose to let go of every one of my fears. I surrender them into your hands.

Lord, I ask you to forgive me for the areas where I have compromised. Today, I choose to stand up for what is right and true.

Lord, where I have been hiding in my comfort zone, I ask you to build my faith.

Lord, you know my worries and anxious thoughts. I give them to you. Please break the worry off my life and flood my heart and mind with your abundant, all-encompassing peace. May the joy of the Lord be my strength.

Lord, today, I choose to forgive those who have hurt and offended me. I release them to you to deal with. Please break every bitter root that has poisoned my life.

Lord, I confess my sins to you and thank you for being faithful and just to forgive and cleanse me. Lord, please break every curse off my life, along with every scheme and snare of the enemy that is sabotaging my life.

Today, I thank you that I am your child. Thank you for setting me free. Lord, I choose to break camp and move forward.

Today, I choose to dare to dream big dreams.

Today, I choose to aim high. Today, I will attempt to do great things with you and for you.

Lord, please help me to reset my goals. Please rekindle a new passion in my heart. Lord, please ignite a new vision in me.

Lord, please help me to be abundantly fruitful.

Lord, please position me in the right place.

Lord, I bring my dreams and plans to you. Please bless me and cause me to prosper.

Please catapult me into my God-ordained destiny.

Lord, I lift the lid.

In Jesus' name, amen.

Today, God has released you from areas in your life that were sabotaging your dreams and holding you back.

Today, you have broken camp. Today, you can start the journey into your God-given destiny.

It is now your time to move forward.

66

***You have stayed at this mountain
long enough.
It is time to break camp
and move on.***

Deuteronomy 1:7-8

Chapter 18

IT'S TIME TO MOVE FORWARD

Get up. Get going. Forward. Onward.
One step at a time.

In the last chapter, we looked at how God told His people who were camped in the wilderness, *"You have stayed at this mountain long enough. It is time to break camp and move on." —Deuteronomy 1:7-8*

God is calling you to break camp, get prepared, arise, and move forward. You need to start dreaming. You need to leave your past behind and move forward into the destiny for which He made you.

What mountains are in your way that are holding you back from God's best?

If you still need to deal with the areas in your life that are sabotaging your dreams, then go back to the previous chapter and deal with them once and for all. The enemy is a dream destroyer. He comes to sap your strength. He comes to sabotage your dreams and ruin your life.

A WORD OF CAUTION

Don't try to move forward without God. Many times, as recorded in the Bible, God's people turned their backs on Him. When they did, they got into all sorts of trouble. Whenever they let go of God, they ended up in sin and bondage. Cut off from God's blessing, they faced captivity, drought, bondage, and pain.

Don't let other things take God's place in your life.

If your life is not right with God, I implore you to surrender to Jesus and make Him the center.

Jesus said, *"Seek the Kingdom of God above all else, and live righteously, and He will give you everything you need." —Matthew 6:33*

THE BIG PICTURE

Just briefly, I want you to look at the big picture.

God wants you to enjoy your life. He wants you to live with purpose and passion. But life consists of more than just the here and now.

So often, we get so consumed with our lives right now that we don't consider our eternity.

On the other end, we often get so caught up in life, haunted by our past, or so worried about tomorrow that we forget to live now. It is time to move forward, away from your past.

We are told, *"This is the day the Lord has made; We will rejoice and be glad in it." —Psalm 118:24*

Make the most of every day. Make the most of today.

Ecclesiastes 11:9 tells us that we need to make the most of life. We are told, *"Enjoy every minute of it. Do everything you want to do; take it all in." —Ecclesiastes 11:9a*

In other words, live your life with passion and purpose. Dare to dream. Aim high.

But it goes on and says, *"But remember that you must give an account to God for everything you do."* — *Ecclesiastes 11:9b*

Live your life to the full! Enjoy it! Take it all in! But remember, there is more to just the life here and now. One day, we will have to appear before God, and each of us will have to give an account to God for everything we do.

God wants you to enjoy your life, but life consists of more than just a few short years on earth.

Life on earth is short, but eternity is forever. Life on earth is temporary, but eternity is permanent.

One day, each one of us will stand before God. There will be a judgment. In eternity, there is a heaven and a hell. Even if you live to be 120, your life on earth is fragile and temporary. But God made you to live forever in his "promised land."

One day, you will die. One day, your heart will stop beating. Still, your spirit will continue to live, either with God in heaven (where there will be no more pain or suffering) or separated from God in hell (where there will be continual torment and pain).

The Bible makes it clear that no one is good enough.

"No one is righteous— not even one." —Romans 3:10

We have all missed the mark.

"For everyone has sinned; we all fall short of God's glorious standard." —Romans 3:23

Sin cuts us off from God's best. Don't let sin rob you of a close walk with God. If you have messed up, then repent of your sins. Don't let your sins mess up your life.

We are told that *"The wages of sin is death."* — *Romans 6:23a*

Sin leads to death and bondage, but here is the good news: although the price of sin leads to death, we are told, *"BUT the free gift of God is eternal life through Christ Jesus our Lord." —Romans 6:23b*

You don't have to live beaten up and condemned for your past sins and transgressions.

Is sin weighing you down?

We are told, *"Let us strip off every weight that slows us down, especially the sin that so easily trips us up. And let us run with endurance the race God has set before us. We do this by keeping our eyes on Jesus, the champion who initiates and perfects our faith. Because of the joy awaiting Him, He endured the cross, disregarding its shame. Now, He is seated in the place of honor beside God's throne. Think of all the hostility He endured from sinful people; then you won't become weary and give up." —Hebrews 12:1-3*

Surrender your life to Jesus. Strip off every weight of sin. Run with endurance. Get your eyes on Jesus.

"If we confess our sins to Him, He is faithful and just to forgive us our sins and to cleanse us from all wickedness." —1 John 1:9

Although sin cuts us off from a holy God, you can confess your sin to God and find complete forgiveness.

"Yet God, in his grace, freely makes us right in his sight. He did this through Christ Jesus when He freed us from the penalty for our sins. For God presented Jesus as the sacrifice for sin. People are made right with God when they believe that Jesus sacrificed his life, shedding his blood." —Romans 3:24

Jesus paid the ultimate price on the cross so that we could find forgiveness. He shed his blood so that we can be set free.

The good news is that God loves you so much. He made a way for all people to be made right with Him so that we could start afresh and be reunited with God, becoming children of God.

If you are not in a relationship with God, call on Jesus today.

If you have drifted from God, you can come back to Him.

If you are weighed down by sin, strip off the weights and set your sights on Jesus.

Today is your day to get reconnected to God.

Call on Jesus to be your Lord and Savior.

"For everyone who calls upon the name of the Lord, will be saved." —Romans 10:13

PRAYER TO SURRENDER YOUR LIFE TO JESUS

Dear Lord Jesus, I need you. I know that I am lost and that I have sinned. I ask for Your forgiveness.

I believe that You died for my sins and rose from the dead. I turn from my sins and invite You into my heart and life. I want to trust and follow You as my Lord and Savior.

In Jesus' name,

Amen.

If you have prayed this prayer, please let us know. We would love to pray for you and send you some incredible resources to help you in your journey with God.

If you have started or restarted your walk with God, welcome to God's family. As a child of God, you can rest assured that your eternity is secure.

You can also live with passion and purpose, knowing that God is with you. He wants to walk the journey with you.

It is now time to move forward with God at your side.

DARE TO DREAM

66

'For I know the plans I have for you,'
says the Lord.
'They are plans for good and not for disaster,
to give you a future and a hope.'

Jeremiah 29:11

Chapter 19
DON'T STOP DREAMING

Don't let go of your hopes and aspirations.

You will have tough times when setting goals and chasing your God-given dreams. But I need to encourage you...

Don't stop dreaming! Don't let go of your hopes and aspirations. Rather, dare to dream!

But, let's be honest, life can be tough. The world seems to have gone crazy. The last few years have been unprecedented. For the first time in the last 40 years, we have had to face a pandemic followed by wars, soaring costs of living, and great polarization. It can be so easy to give up on your dreams when you look at the instability and chaos around the world. And due to the current economic events, many are certainly not thriving but rather battling to survive.

In our current times of distress, it is easy to get despondent, live in fear, worry, and want to give in.

It is easy to let go of your dreams and ask, "What's the point?"

When you face tough times, it can stop you from dreaming. It is easy to let go of your dreams when challenges arise.

We are living in dark days, and there are many

challenges ahead.

But you need to stay positive. You need to look forward. You need to look up. Lift the lid!

If you are facing a crisis, I need to tell you...

Hold on.

There is a Savior. He came to save you. He came to rescue you.

There is hope.

Even though the world seems to be getting darker and darker, there is still hope in God.

God is still on the throne.

He has all power and authority in heaven and on earth.

You may have lost your way. You may have let go of your dreams. You may want to give up or give in.

But it is time to rise. It is time to look up. It is time to look to Jesus.

Don't let hard knocks stop you from dreaming! Don't let your dreams be ruined.

If you are worried, living in fear, or if you have let go of your dreams, I implore you to put your hope in God.

God made you with a destiny to fulfill.

DON'T LET THE DREAM DESTROYER LURE YOU AWAY FROM YOUR DESTINY

The dream destroyer will try to turn your dreams into dread and will try to lead you into bondage.

According to Jesus, the enemy (aka the dream destroyer) *"comes to kill, steal, and destroy,"* but Jesus (our Savior) came to *"Bring you life and life more abundantly." —John 10:10*

God knows what is happening. He knows you through and through. He knows your name, and *"The very hairs on your head are numbered." —Luke 12:7*

God sees your struggles, your frustrations, your disappointments. He sees it all.

God has not given up on you. Don't give up on Him. Keep dreaming.

Giving up on your dreams is so easy when you face a crisis. It's so easy to let go of your passion and your purpose.

Don't give up on your dreams. Don't accept the current crisis as your lot in life.

It is time to arise. You can dare to dream.

God made you, and He doesn't make junk. God wants the best for you. He is for you and made you to be alive at this current time. He still has a plan for your life. He can still cause everything to work out for the good.

Even in the middle of the current chaos and crisis, you need to keep dreaming.

Dare to dream. Aim high. Attempt great things with God.

God still has a plan for you. Do you believe this?

Many do not believe this. But God does have plans for you, and *"They are plans for good and not for disaster, to give you a future and a hope." —Jeremiah 29:11*

God has an eternal plan. He made you to live forever. Yes, in eternity, there is a heaven and a hell.

We will all spend eternity either with God or separated from Him.

Don't forget Jesus. He paid the full price on the cross so that you and I can spend eternity with Him. Don't ever think that God doesn't have a good plan for you.

Don't stop dreaming.

It is time to dare to dream and reset your goals. It is time to rekindle your passion and to live on purpose. It is time to reignite your vision. It is time to attempt great things with and for God. It is time to get positioned for God to catapult you into your destiny. It is time to be fruitful.

Dream.

Plan.

Set up a strategy.

Follow through.

Your best days are ahead of you!

It is time to DARE TO DREAM!

DARE TO DREAM

About
THE AUTHOR

Clinton lives in Noordhoek, in the southern peninsula of Cape Town, nestled between two oceans. He is married to his beautiful wife, Janet, and has four sons.

He is the CEO of Invest 4 Life. He has been in the financial planning industry for over 30 years, specializing in helping people manage their money well, emphasizing generating wealth and building towards financial freedom. He has been involved in various leadership positions over the years.

Clinton also presents weekly radio shows on CCFM, the second-largest Christian station in South Africa. One of the programs he presents, Financial Matters, has helped thousands manage their money better. At the same time, hundreds respond to the Good News of Jesus Christ every month on Time to Decide and find new life.

Clinton also writes a weekly blog called **betteryouliving.com,** that aims to reach the lost, bring hope to the hurting, and inspire people to live their best lives now with an eye on eternity. Over the years, tens of thousands have responded to accept Jesus as their Lord and Savior, with millions being influenced through its social media presence.

About
BETTER **YOU** LIVING

From what started as a simple Instagram page in July 2020, Better**You**Living has grown to astronomical heights across all platforms.

Run by father-son duo, Clinton and Josh Werner, their social media presence, and blogs aim to offer hope, godly wisdom, and encouragement, reaching many for Christ.

Feel free to **join us** on our social media **(@betteryouliving)** and blog **(betteryouliving.com)** to be inspired and see the amazing things God is doing. We want to see you grow in your walk with God and live the life He has called you to.

May God bless you abundantly.

NOTES

CHAPTER 1: LIFT THE LID
1. Proverbs 13:12 NLT
2. Cape Town's 2023 population is now estimated at 4,890,280. These population estimates and projections come from the latest revision of the UN World Urbanization Prospects (worldpopulationreview.com/world-cities/cape-town-population#Cape%20Town%20Demographics).
3. Quarterly Labour Force Survey Quarter 3: 2023 (https://www.statssa.gov.za/ quarterly Labour Force Survey Quarter 3: 2023)

CHAPTER 2: TIME TO FLY
1. Isaiah 40:31 NLT
2. The Eagle Who Thought He Was a Chicken - A Story About Our Identity (billjohnsononline.com), Bill Johnson (07/12/2017)
3. Isaiah 40:27
4. Isaiah 40:29
5. Isaiah 40:30-31
6. Jeremiah 29:11
7. Jeremiah 29:12-13
8. Psalms 113:5-8
9. Isaiah 40:30-31

CHAPTER 3: A FRESH START
1. Isaiah 43:19 NLT
2. Ecclesiastes 3:1
3. Jeremiah 29:11
4. Romans 8:28

CHAPTER 4: JUMP!
1. Matthew 14:28-29 Message
2. Fleas in a jar (similarity in fleas and human behaviour) — YouTube - MMM Global School - May 3, 2015
3. You are a flea in a jar — Unbounded (be-unbounded.com)
4. Matthew 19:26
5. Matthew 14:24-34

CHAPTER 5: GOD CAN BRING YOUR DEAD DREAMS BACK TO LIFE
1. John 10:10 NLT
2. Matthew 11:28
3. John 11:23
4. John 11:25-26
5. John 11:39
6. John 11:40-44
7. Hebrews 13:8
8. Luke 1:37
9. Jeremiah 32:27
10. Isaiah 43:19
11. John 1:12
12. John 8:36

CHAPTER 6 - FRESH VISION
1. Mark 10:52 NLT
2. John 10:10
3. Mark 10:48
4. Mark 10:51-52

CHAPTER 7 - SETBACKS AND COMEBACKS
1. Genesis 39:2
2. Genesis 37:9 NLT
3. Genesis 37:31-32 NLT
4. Genesis 37:36 NLT
5. Genesis 39:2-6 NLT
6. Genesis 39:10-12 NLT
7. Genesis 39:14-15 NLT
8. Genesis 39:19-23 NLT

9. Genesis 40:13-14 NLT
10. Genesis 40:19-23 NLT
11. Genesis 41:11-13 NLT
12. Genesis 41:15-17 NLT
13. Genesis 41:25-30 NLT
14. Genesis 41:36-41 NLT
15. Genesis 41:44 NLT
16. Genesis 41:47-49 NLT

17. Genesis 41:54-57 NLT
18. Genesis 42:5-6 NLT
19. Genesis 42:8-9 NLT
20. Genesis 45:4-11 NLT
21. John 16:33 NIV
22. Psalm 23:4 NIV
23. Isaiah 43:2
24. John 15:5 NV
25. John 3:16 NIV
26. Romans 10:13 NIV
27. Matthew 28:20 NLT
28. Philippians 4:13 NLT
29. Romans 8:28 NLT
30. Philippians 4:19 NIV
31. Romans 8:37 NLT
32. Isaiah 43:19

CHAPTER 8 - EXTRAORDINARY

1. Colossians 3:23
2. Albert Einstein quote
3. Craig Groeschel quote
4. Dave Ramsey quote
5. Brain Tracy quote
6. Psalm 3:5-6
7. Dave Ramsey quote
8. John Maxwell quote

CHAPTER 9 - PICTURE. PLAN. PROCESS.

1. Isaiah 43:19 NLT
2. Proverbs 13:12 NLT
3. Proverbs 29:18
4. Proverbs 21:5
5. Proverbs 24:3-4

CHAPTER 10 - GOOD PLANNING LEADS TO SUCCESS

1. Proverbs 21:5
2. 1 Kings 3:5
3. 1 Kings 3:9-10
4. 1 Kings 3:11-14
5. 1 Kings 4:20

6. 1 Kings 4:25
7. Proverbs 21:5 NIV

CHAPTER 11 - THE POWER OF SETTING GOALS
1. Habakkuk 2:2
2. Proverbs 13:12

CHAPTER 12 - YOUR GOAL-SETTING PLAN
1. Psalm 20:4
2. Proverbs 13:12
3. Habakkuk 2:2
4. Proverbs 29:18
5. Proverbs 21:5
6. Proverbs 10:4
7. Proverbs 13:4

CHAPTER 13 - THE SYSTEM
1. Ecclesiastes 7:8
2. Proverbs 21:5
3. Ecclesiastes 3:1-3
4. Ecclesiastes 10:2
5. Atomic Habits, which I recommend you read to form good habits, James Clear.

CHAPTER 14 - THE MISSING KEY
1. Proverbs 16:3
2. Psalm 37:3-4
3. Psalm 37:3-5
4. 1 Chronicles 4:9-10
5. Psalm 103:13
6. James 1:5
7. James 4:2
8. Matthew 7:7-8
9. John 16:24
10. Proverbs 23:4
11. Psalm 19:21
12. Psalm 127:1
13. Philippians 4:13
14. Isaiah 43:19
15. Deuteronomy 8:18

CHAPTER 15 - REVIEW
1. Proverbs 27:23-24

CHAPTER 16 - PUT YOUR PLANS INTO PRACTICE
1. Psalm 37:4
2. Proverbs 29:18
3. Ecclesiastes 3:1
4. Proverbs 21:5
5. Ecclesiastes 7:8
6. Proverbs 16:3
7. Psalm 37:3-5
8. Proverbs 27:23

CHAPTER 18 - DON'T LET GO OF YOUR DESTINY
1. James 1:12 NIV
2. Genesis 11:31-32 NLT
3. Genesis 12:1
4. Genesis 12:2-3
5. Genesis 12:4
6. Genesis15:1
7. Genesis15:2
8. Genesis15:5-6
9. Genesis 15:7

CHAPTER 19 - IT'S TIME TO BREAK CAMP
1. Philippians 3:13-14 NIV
2. Exodus 2:23-25
3. Exodus 10:23
4. Deuteronomy 1:2
5. Joshua 5:6
6. Joel 2:25
7. Deuteronomy 1:7
8. Deuteronomy 1:8
9. John 8:32
10. Numbers 13:27 NLT
11. Numbers 13:28 NLT
12. Numbers 13:31-33 NLT
13. Numbers 13:30 NLT

14.Isaiah 41:10
15.Joshua 1:9
16.Matthew 24:12
17.Matthew 24:13
18.Proverbs 12:25
19.Philippians 4:6-7
20.Matthew 11:28
21.Matthew 6:14-15
22.Matthew 11:22-24
23.Mark 11:25

CHAPTER 20 - IT'S TIME TO MOVE FORWARD
1. Deuteronomy 1:7-8 NIV
2. John 10:10
3. Matthew 6:33
4. Psalm 118:24
5. Ecclesiastes 11:9
6. Romans 3:10
7. Romans 3:23
8. Romans 6:23
9. Hebrews 12:1-3
10.1 John 1:9
11. Romans 3:24
12.Romans 10:13

CHAPTER 17 - DON'T STOP DREAMING
1. Jeremiah 29:11
2. John 10:10
3. Luke 12:7

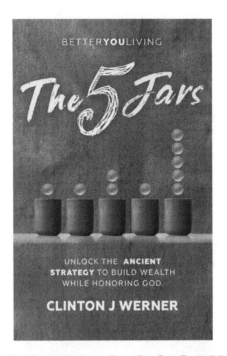

COMING SOON!

If you enjoyed **DARE TO DREAM**, I'm sure you'll love our upcoming project, **'THE 5 JARS'**, where we'll be unpacking a strategy that has been **passed down from ancient generations** to help you build wealth while honoring God. It will even be great for children, teaching them Biblical principles to live by that will put God at the center and ensure that they receive financial wisdom to help them prosper.

If you are interested, join the waiting list by visiting the **resources page** on **betteryouliving.com**.

CLINTON J WERNER

Made in the USA
Columbia, SC
25 September 2024